RUSSIAN
FOLK
LYRICS

RUSSIAN
FOLK
LYRICS

TRANSLATED AND EDITED BY

ROBERTA REEDER

WITH AN INTRODUCTORY ESSAY BY

V. JA. PROPP

INDIANA UNIVERSITY PRESS

Bloomington and Indianapolis

Library of Congress Cataloging-in-Publication Data

Russian folk lyrics / translated and edited by Roberta Reeder ; with
an introductory essay by V. Ja. Propp.
    p. cm.
    Rev. and enl. ed. of Down along the Mother Volga. 1975.
    The introductory essay by Propp is a new translation of O russkoĭ
narodnoĭ liricheskoĭ pesne, which was originally published in
Narodnye liricheskie pesni, 1961.
    Includes bibliographical references and indexes.
    ISBN 0-253-34623-1 (cloth). — ISBN 0-253-20749-5 (pbk.)
    1. Folk-songs, Russian—Soviet Union—Texts. I. Reeder, Roberta.
II. Propp, V. IA. (Vladimir IAkovlevich), 1895–1970. III. Propp,
V. IA. (Vladimir IAkovlevich), 1895–1970. O russkoĭ narodnoĭ
liricheskoĭ pesne. English. 1992. IV. Down along the Mother
Volga.
PG3140.D6 1992
398.2'0947—dc20   92-7155

1 2 3 4 5   96 95 94 93

To Michael

Contents

Preface

The presentation here of V. Ja. Propp's analysis of the Russian folk lyric makes available a significant contribution by this noted scholar to the study of folklore. His earlier work, *The Morphology of the Folktale*, which has been translated into many languages, has become a landmark in the structural analysis of various folklore genres. In his study of Russian folk lyrics, Propp does not limit himself to formalistic analysis, but also relates them to the social and historical context in which they were produced. Propp's study is supplemented by a comprehensive anthology of typical examples from the various genres of the Russian folk lyric. Through the beliefs and attitudes reflected in these songs, one may find in this publication a wealth of material useful to anthropologists, historians, and literary scholars.

V. Ja. Propp's work, "O russkoj narodnoj liričeskoj pesne" [The Russian Folk Lyric], appears in his anthology *Narodnye liričeskie pesni* [Lyric Folk Songs], ed. V. Ja. Propp, 2d ed., Biblioteka poèta, bol'šaja serija (Leningrad: Sovetskij pisatel', 1961), pp. 5–68. I have translated from this anthology those lyrics which I considered most representative of each particular type, and I have supplemented these with selections from I. I. Zemcovskij, ed., *Poèzija krest'janskix prazdnikov* [The Poetry of Peasant Festivals], 2d ed., Biblioteka poèta, bol'šaja serija (Leningrad: Sovetskij pisatel' 1970) and N.P. Kolpakova, ed., *Lirika russkoj svad'by* [Lyrics of the Russian Wedding] (Leningrad: Nauka, 1973). The Sources of Folk Lyrics which appears after the anthology comes from Propp's edition. The asterisks within Propp's essay refer to his own notes, and the numbered footnotes refer to my notes which appear at the end of the text. I have transliterated according to the following transliteration system:

А	а	a		Р	р	r
Б	б	b		С	с	s
В	в	v		Т	т	t
Г	г	g		У	у	u
Д	д	d		Ф	ф	f
Е	е	e		Х	х	x
Ё	ё	ё		Ц	ц	c
Ж	ж	ž		Ч	ч	č
З	з	z		Ш	ш	š
И	и	i		Щ	щ	šč
Й	й	j		Ъ	ъ	"
К	к	k		Ы	ы	y
Л	л	l		Ь	ь	'
М	м	m		Э	э	è
Н	н	n		Ю	ю	ju
О	о	o		Я	я	ja
П	п	p				

Exception is made for anglicized words such as ruble, Moscow, and tsar, for references to works in English concerning Russian material, and to familiar names such as Tolstoy and Pushkin.

Among the many friends and colleagues who have helped me make this book possible, I offer special thanks to James Bailey, Felix Oinas, J. T. Shaw, Munro Edmonson, Anatole Pohorilenko, Marianne Osborne, and June Pachuta. I should also like to thank the Stanford University Press for permission to reproduce the diagram "Basic Plans of Peasant Houses in Nineteenth-Century Russia" and Holt, Rinehart, and Winston, Inc., for their permission to reproduce the map of central Russia.

I am grateful to Pauline Lewin for all her help in preparing V. Ja. Propp's introduction.

ROBERTA REEDER

Editor's Introduction

The difficulties of translating folk lyrics from Russian have been multiplied by conventions of syntax, lexicon, and grammar which differ from the standard literary language and which add a special richness and quality peculiar to this poetry. Without going into elaborate detail, I should like to make the non-Russian reader aware of some of the possibilities provided by the linguistic conventions used in these lyrics.

One of the characteristics of the syntax of a Russian folk lyric is the repetition of prepositions:[1] "Kak *na* ètoj *na* krovati" (*on* this *on* bed), "kak *vo* gorode *vo* Ustjužine" (*in* the city *in* Ustjužin). This syntax is not obligatory, and often the same song will use the syntax conventional to the literary language, that is, preposition plus all the components following at once within the prepositional phrase. For example, in the song "kak vo gorode vo Ustjužine" we also see the phrase "po tëmnym lesam" (along the dark forests) instead of "*po* tëmnym *po* lesam." A literal translation of the repeated prepositions would sound awkward, and I have translated these phrases into normal English syntax, without the repetition.

Another problem in the translation of Russian folk lyrics is the frequency of the occurrence of diminutives, which give a subjective nuance to the object referred to, usually by adding an endearing or a derogatory connotation to the word. Where this nuance seemed important, I have translated the word with "dear," "little," or in other cases, "nasty." For example:

> Ty proščaj že, rodinaja,
> Nenagljadnoe *solnyško!*

---

[1]Repetition of prepositions is found not only in folklore, but also in Old Church Slavic and Old Russian texts, and can be seen in several Russian dialects. For an analysis of the repetition of prepositions in the *bylina*, see Roy G. Jones, *Language and Prosody of the Russian Folk Epic* (The Hague, 1972), pp. 55–64. Felix J. Oinas, in "Concord in Balto-Finnic and Preposition Repetition in Russian," *American Studies in Uralic Linguistics* (Indiana University Publications, Uralic and Altaic Series, I; Bloomington, Indiana, 1960), pp. 121–138, reviews some of the theories concerning the repetition of prepositions in Russian folklore; Ju. M. Sokolov suggests this occurs in the *bylina* as a means of retardation; A. A. Shaxmatov explains it as an indication of concord between the modifier and the word modified; V. I. Sobinnikova says that repetition "creates the predicativeness, at the same time preserving the attributiveness." An example is *iz bistru is pustova* (from the bead from the hollow one), which could be interpreted as *iz bistru, kotoryj byl pustym* (from the bead which was hollow) (p. 130). N. P. Grinkova provides another explanation. According to her, repetition is a means of emphasizing words that are important semantically. In the example *u Gavrili u 'djaka* (by Gavril, by the deacon), the second preposition *u* stresses the fact that this is about Gavril the deacon, and not about any other Gavril (p. 131). Oinas comes to the conclusion that these various explanations are not mutually exclusive, that they represent different aspects of the function of the repetition of prepositions.

> Goodby, my own,
> Beloved *little sun.*

Here "solnyško" instead of the usual "solnce" implies the love the girl feels for her mother, whom she refers to here as "sun." I have also kept the diminutive where it adds variety to a line, for example, *"dolinuška"* for *"dolina"* (valley).

> Dolina l' ty moja, *dolinuška,*
> Dolina l' ty širokaja!

> You valley of mine, *little valley,*
> You valley so wide!

Another convention of the syntax of the Russian folk lyric is placing the adjective after the noun. As A. P. Evgen'eva points out,[2] the norm in the contemporary literary language is to have the adjective precede the noun, while in the Russian oral tradition the adjective often comes after, emphasizing a certain quality of the given noun. Often this is difficult to translate into English. For example:

> Vyrastala trava šëlkovaja,
> Rascveli, rascveli,
> Rascveli cvety lazorevye.

literally is:

> There grew grass silken,
> There bloomed, there bloomed,
> There bloomed flowers azure.

Pleonasms are often difficult to translate as well. For example:

> On ni *nočen'ki* doma ne *nočuet,*

where *nočuet* means "to spend the night" and *nočen'ki* "nights"; translated literally the above results in "he did not 'night' the 'nights' at home." Occasionally there are equivalent pleonasms in English, for example, "zasnyla sny" ("dreamt dreams") works well.

Another convention of Russian oral poetry is the use of synonym pairs, which Evgen'eva sees as forming a new complex word: "gljažu-smotrju" (glance-look); "mesjac-luna" (moon-moon), where the second synonym comes from French. Such pairs come from all grammatical categories— verbs, nouns, adjectives, and so forth. Stylistically they give strength

---

[2]A. P. Evgen'eva, *Očerki po jazyku russkoj ustnoj poèzii* [A Study of the Language of Russian Oral Poetry] (Moscow-Leningrad, 1963), p. 54.

and nuance to the meaning, emphasizing it. When these combinations
appear, I keep as closely to the original synonym-complex as possible.
For example: "Carev syn xoroběr/ Da ty čto xodiš'-guljaeš'?" becomes
"Why are you walking-strolling?" and "Mimo sadu-vinogradu" becomes "By the garden-vineyard."

The last convention I would like to mention is one that is stylistically
fascinating in Russian but difficult to translate. This is the use of a noun
in one line and the adjective modifying it in the next, usually in parallel
position:

> Ne radujtes', duby,
> Ne radujtes' zelënye!

literally translates as:

> Don't rejoice oaks,
> Don't rejoice green!

A similar problem is the convention of putting someone's first name in
one line, and their patronymic in the next, again in parallel position:

> "Ty ne plač', ne plač', Avdot'juška,
> Ty ne plač', duša Vasil'evna!"

where the girl is usually referred to as Avdot'ja Vasil'evna.

These are only some of the difficulties in "being faithful" to the Russian folk lyric.[3] In addition, there are problems of lexicon, words which
are not part of the standard vocabulary of the literary language, and
problems of dialectical grammatical constructions. There are also the
ordinary problems one generally meets in translating Russian into English, such as the lack of articles in Russian and the free distribution of
word order within a sentence, which is difficult or impossible to produce
in an English sentence with its relatively fixed word order.

As an illustration of the type of problem one encounters as a translator
of Russian folk lyrics, I quote the song "Na gory" with both a literal
translation and one that is more poetic.

> Na gorý, na gorý da zelënyj sad;
> V ètom sadu v tom zelenóm
> Pëtro guljal da Vasil'evič,
> Česal golovú, zavival kudrí,
> Nadeval čuločki bely šëlkovye,
> Obuval bašmački da so prjažečkami;

---

[3]For a discussion of other aspects of differences in the language of the Russian folk
lyric from normal literary speech, see D. P. Costello and I. P. Foote, eds., "The Language
of Folk Literature," *Russian Folk Literature* (Oxford, 1967), pp. xi–xvii.

Celoval-miloval Stepanidu-dušú:
"Ty drug moja Stepanida-duša!
Ty drug moja, Oxromeevna!"

Translated literally it is:

On the mountain, on the mountain is a green garden;
In this garden in this green
Pëtro was walking, yes, Vasil'evič,
Combed head, twisted curls,
Put on stockings white silken,
Put on boots, yes, with buckles;
Kissed-caressed Stepanida-darling:
"You are sweetheart my, Stepanida-darling!
"Your are sweetheart my, Oxromeevna!"

Translated into good English, it would be:

On the mountain, on the mountain is a green garden;
In this garden, this green garden
Pëtro was walking, Pëtro Vasil'evič,
He combed his hair, twisted his curls,
Put on white silken stockings,
Put on boots with buckles;
He kissed and caressed Stepanida-darling:
"You are my sweetheart, Stepanida-darling!
You are my sweetheart, Stepanida Oxromeevna!"

Fig. 1   Map of Central Russia. From THE PEASANTS OF CENTRAL
RUSSIA by Stephen P. Dunn and Ethel Dunn. Copyright © 1967
by Holt, Rinehart and Winston, Inc. Reprinted by permission of
Holt, Rinehart and Winston, Inc.

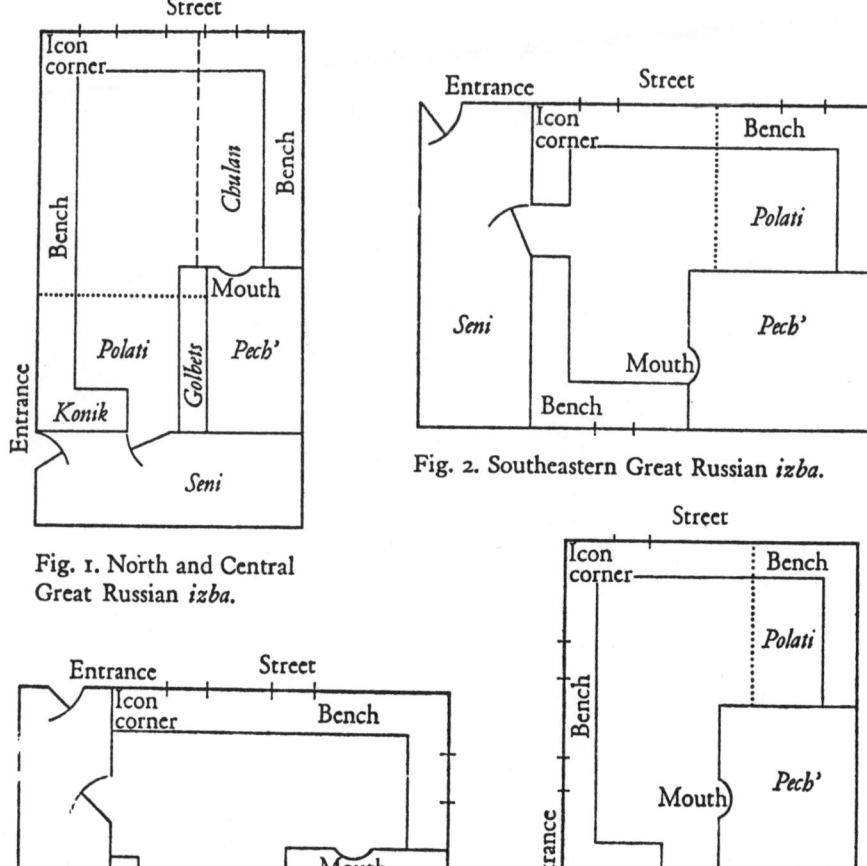

Fig. 1. North and Central
Great Russian *izba*.

Fig. 2. Southeastern Great Russian *izba*.

Fig. 3. Southwestern Great Russian *izba*.

Fig. 4. *Khata* of Western
Great Russia, Belorussia
and the Ukraine.

Fig. 2   Basic Plans of Peasant Houses in Nineteenth-Century Russia.
From "The Peasant Way of Life," by Mary Matossian: THE
PEASANT IN NINETEENTH-CENTURY RUSSIA, edited by
W. S. Vucinich. Copyright © 1968 by Stanford University Press.
Reprinted by permission of Stanford University Press.

RUSSIAN
FOLK
LYRICS

The Russian Folk lyric

V. Ja. Propp
Translated by Roberta Reeder

I

In order to gain a true understanding of folk song one must keep in mind
that the songs created by the folk were never intended to be read, and
they should not be examined the same way as written poems are. They
also do not resemble romances—poems set to music by composers. In
a genuine folk song the melody and words form an original, organic, and
indivisible whole. Both aspects represent an important part of Russian
folk culture. Even without taking the melody into account, the literary
content of folk songs is so significant, varied, and beautiful that it
deserves extensive study on its own, although this type of study alone
would provide an incomplete picture of the essence of Russian song.

The first transcriptions of Russian folk songs go back to the seventeenth century, but extensive collections intended for the general public
did not appear before the second half of the eighteenth century, and
scholarly collecting of folk songs began only in the nineteenth century.
Excellent collections were published and produced by admirers of folk
songs—folklorists, linguists, ethnographers, and composers. Methods of
transcription and publication were gradually perfected. The most important nonritual folk lyrics which had appeared in print were edited and
reprinted in 1895–1902 by A. I. Sobolevsky.* Although this collection is
not complete, it provides a broad picture of the Russian folk lyric in the
eighteenth and nineteenth centuries. Since it appeared, the quantity of
material collected and published has continued to grow. An enormous
amount has been collected in the Soviet period. The amount of collected
material, both published and preserved in the archives, is tremendous.
It is not the lack of material, but the abundance of it that has made
research difficult.

An enormous number of songs have not yet been categorized. We
require a system that would provide a proper way of presenting the rich
ideological and historical content of the song—a presentation that would
illuminate what the folk expressed in song. The word "lyric" could be
interpreted in the narrow sense as the poetic expression of profoundly
individual emotions. This is not an appropriate definition for folklore.

---

*A. I. Sobolevskij, ed., *Velikorusskie narodnye pesni* [Great-Russian Folk Songs], 7 vols.
(St. Petersburg, 1895–1902).

A broader understanding of the word would be more useful here, since in folklore individual feelings are related to collective ones. Lyric songs include not only love songs but also songs reflecting varied social content.

From a formal point of view the song material could be classified in a number of ways, which might at first appear to be correct. Thus, based on the tempo in which songs are performed, they may be divided into *protjažnye* (largo), semilargo, and *častye* (allegro); this type of classification appears in song books with musical accompaniment at the beginning of the nineteenth century.

On the basis of their application to community life, songs may be classified as work songs, wedding songs, Yuletide songs, etc. Musicologists may divide songs according to musical distinctions. However, what is needed are categories that would express the essence of a song and would show the basic distinctive features of its type.

One of the most important features of a folk song is the social class it reflects. From this point of view, all folk lyrics may be divided into two basic types: the songs of the peasants and the songs of the workers. However, the prerevolutionary peasantry was not a monolithic whole. It was composed of various strata which created songs that were sometimes very different. The songs should first be divided into those directly related to peasants, to their work connected with the soil; most Russian lyric folk songs fall into this category. The peasant lyrics in turn may be divided into two basic types: ritual and nonritual. Ritual lyrics can then be divided into calendar-ritual songs or family songs: wedding songs or funeral laments. The nonritual lyric may be studied according to its subject matter and the way in which it is performed.

The peasantry was also composed of people who were torn away, voluntarily or not, from agicultural labor. Their songs had a very different content: barge hauler songs, soldier songs, robber songs, prison, and labor camp songs all belong to this category. With the rise of the factory proletariat, the workers' songs appear—one of the types of songs characterized by increasing revolutionary sentiment.

In many cases the class affiliation determines the poetics as well. For example, in every respect the barge-hauler songs are quite different from the love songs of peasant girls. Soldier songs have nothing in common with bridal laments, and so on. Thus to a certain degree the social content also determines the artistic nature of songs, since different subject matter determines a difference in form.

II

Different types of songs have different historical roots. In studying folk song from the historical point of view, it is necessary to begin with its most ancient genres. Ritual agricultural poetry is one of the oldest types of folk lyric.[1] These songs accompanied the performance of certain rites which took place on particular days of the calendar to promote the fertility of the earth and cattle, and the health and prosperity of the people. Instead of using the official state and church lunar calendar, the early farmer calculated time according to the solar calendar. The solar new year began with the winter solstice. The church established this day—the day of the new birth of the sun—as the day of the birth of Christ; however, artificially imposed Christian holidays could not force out the old, joyful pagan holidays.

In the villages on Christmas Eve the peasants sang a special song called *koljada* or *koljadka*.[2] The word is etymologically related to the word *calendae* (Greek *xalandai*), the designation given by the ancient Romans to the first ten days of every month. The word "calendar" comes from this root. In folk usage the word has several different meanings: it can designate the time period of the holiday; it may refer to the songs ("to sing a *koljada*"); it may designate a certain living being ("*koljada* was born on Christmas Eve"). *Koljadas* were not sung by a solo voice but by a merry band of young people who went from hut to hut, asked permission of the host to sing a *koljada*, and then performed it. The content of Russian *koljadas* is generally the same. Basically the song is composed of a narrative telling how the singers had been looking for the host's *dvor*[3] and how they found it. This is followed by praising and extolling the host, the hostess, and their children, and the song ends with a suggestion to the host to send some tarts or pancakes out to the young people: this present is also sometimes called a *koljada*. If the present is good, the singers sing a new song, promising the hosts a rich harvest, but if the host turns out to be stingy, they shower him with comic abuse and promise him all kinds of misery and misfortune.

Koljadas were mainly popular in central Russia. In the Volga area and in certain other places the word is unknown; the word *ovsen'* (*tausen'*, *usen'*) corresponds to it. The etymology of the word is not completely clear. On the one hand, it may be associated with the root *ves*, meaning "light" (compare *vesna* [spring]); on the other hand, it may go back to roots connected with the words *ovës* [oats], the first known grain, and *sev* [sowing]. Neither interpretation is incompatible with the content and meaning of the songs.

The magic power of influencing reality was once ascribed to *koljadas*. With the loss of this belief, singing *koljadas* turned into a merry game. The game consisted not only of singing *koljadas* but also of imitating ploughing and sowing, leading a goat and performing different scenes with it, leading a bear, mummery, and various games in peasant huts, during which game songs were sung.*

---

*The latest research done on this cycle is: V. I. Čičerov, *Zimnij period russkogo narod-

On New Year's fortunes were told. Poetic folklore accompanied only one type of fortune telling: Young girls would drop their rings into a bowl of water, which was covered by a towel. Short songs were then sung, allegorically revealing what awaited the girls: marriage, an extension of maidenhood, separation, a journey, riches, death, and so on. These songs were called *podbljudnaja* [under the plate] songs.[4] With each song one ring was taken out, and the song and the fate it foretold applied to the girl to whom the ring belonged. The *podbljudnaja* songs are very poetic. Pushkin transcribed one of them and used it in *Eugene Onegin* (chapter 5, stanza 8). In their allegorical nature they resemble riddles; they are rich in folk metaphors and are valuable for studying imagery typical of folklore in particular. Like *koljadas*, one type of *podbljudnaja* song is related to praise songs. In these songs the refrain "glory" is sung after each line.

The holiday following Yuletide was Carnival [*Maslenica*].[5] Carnival preceded Lent, and the folk tried to enjoy themselves as much as possible until its arrival. However, Maslenica rituals cannot be explained by this alone. These rituals are the remnants of an ancient agricultural religion of the death and resurrection of a deity. In the spring the god of vegetation was slain in order to ensure his resurrection and to summon new vegetation. This religion was characteristic of the agricultural peoples of the ancient Orient, of antiquity, and of Europe. The central ritual consisted of welcoming and saying farewell to the deity Maslenica, who was portrayed as an effigy made of straw or rags. It was led with laughter, jokes, and merry songs on a barrow or wagon, or in a sleigh to the village; toward the end of Carnival week the effigy was led out beyond the village and, with merry jokes, torn apart, burned, and thrown into the field. Accompanying the slaying of the god with laughter had a particular significance: it was assumed that such a death led toward life.[*] Very few Carnival songs have been preserved. Their subject matter concerns the humorous banishment of Carnival.

The vernal equinox (around 22 March) represents the beginning of spring. The ancient farmer did not yet understand the regularity of natural phenomena and assumed that spring had to be invoked, that is, that invocations would summon her to life or help her appear. In spring the birds would come, and the peasants thought that the birds brought spring with them.[6] The invocations to spring have the form of an address to

nogo zemledel'českogo kalendarja XVI-XIX vekov [The Winter Period of the Russian Folk Agricultural Calendar of the Sixteenth–Nineteenth Centuries] (Očerki po istorii narodnyx verovanij) [Essays on the History of Folk Beliefs], Trudy Instituta ètnografii AN SSSR [Transactions of the Institute of Ethnography AN USSR], new series, vol. 40 (Moscow, 1957).

  [*]V. Propp, "Ritual'nyj smex v fol'klore" [Ritual Laughter in Folklore], Učënye zapiski Leningradskogo universiteta [Scholarly Notes, Leningrad University], no. 46 (Leningrad, 1939).

birds. All these concepts were forgotten long ago, and invocations to spring were transformed into children's games. The children baked pastry in the form of birds, saying, "The rooks have come," and tossed them up into the air or tied them to poles in the garden. This was done to portray (and, consequently, summon) the coming of the birds and the arrival of spring. The songs sung for this occasion were commonly called *vesnjanki* [spring songs]. They reflect the troubles and strivings of the peasantry, and some of them express the joy of spring and celebrate it poetically.[7] On this day birds were let out of their cages—a custom celebrated in verse by Pushkin.[8]

After the welcoming of spring, or from the first Sunday after Easter (this day is called "Beautiful [red] hillock"),[9] the performance of *xorovods* began. *Xorovod* songs are not always ritual songs, but like them, they enter into the general stream of spring festivities. The majority are devoted to love, and cheerful, joyful songs predominate. It is quite probable that the erotic content of spring *xorovod* songs was related to concepts concerning the earth's fertility. These concepts disappeared long ago. Besides love songs, there are also strictly agricultural labor songs which directly express the desire for a good harvest.

One of the most widespread spring game songs is about sowing flax (#23). The female performer would stand in the middle of a circle and portray in mime how the flax was sown, pulled, spread out, and so on, right up to the spinning of the yarn. The imitation of labor (imitative or simulated magic) supposedly promoted its productivity. The refrain, "Turn out well, turn out well, my flax, turn out well, my white flax," expressed only wishful sentiments in the eighteenth and nineteenth centuries, but in earlier times similar refrains or songs had invocatory significance.

The famous song "Oh, millet we have sown" (#22) belongs to this category. The song is primarily a love game, the capture of a girl by young men. It is one of the oldest Russian songs, and its melodies were transcribed or used by Balakirev, Rimsky-Korsakov, Tchaikovsky, Taneev, and Kastalsky.[10]

Springtime* passes quickly: everything appears before one's very eyes; the earth quickly turns green. The March invocations to spring are barely heard when the time comes to drive the flocks out to the field—"George-Egorij with silken grass" arrives. The flocks are driven out on St. George's day,** in April, with a pussy willow left from Palm Sunday.† They sing a song about the willow: "The pussy willow has

---

*This section, on St. George's Day, through p. 7, was taken from I. I. Zemcovskij, ed., *Poezija krest' janskix prazdnikov.* Bol'šaja serija, 2d ed. (Leningrad: Sovetskij pisatel', 1970), pp. 27–28.

**The name Egorij derives from the Greek name George, which literally means "farmer." The timing of the first driving out of the flocks into the fields on this day was expressed in the refrain "Egor'juška-zagonuška" (Egorushka—the driver), Zemcovskij, p. 27.

†In a Russian folk custom, on Palm Sunday people lightly whip each other with willows.

brought health! A pussy willow whip beats you to tears, the pretty pussy willow does not beat in vain!" The entire village, from very young to very old, all gather together—it is a solemn, long-awaited moment. As soon as the flocks leave the village, some of the pussy willow branches are stuck into the rye field, transmitting their spring vegetative strength to it, and some are taken home to ensure that the flocks will return. Men predominate on this holiday. Old men take as many stones from the river as they have animals in their flock, sew them in a bag, and put them in the courtyard, saying:

> Tsar of the field, tsaritsa of the field,
> Tsar of the forest, tsaritsa of the forest,
> Tsar of the water, tsaritsa of the water!
> All twigs and sticks
> Protect my flocks,
> From the evil eye, from wicked people,
> From wild beasts and from all others.*

They walk around the field singing invocations to St. George, begging him to protect the flocks "in the fields and beyond the fields" from all cunning beasts. On the eve of driving out the flocks, young boys (or men) walk around the village and sing in front of each house, addressing the host as in the rituals. The singers chant:

> Cows, give birth to calves!
> Pigs, give birth to sucklings!
> Roosters, stamp your feet!
> Hens, hatch chickens!
> Hostess, be good to us!
> Host, don't be stingy!

And if an award is given "for labor on St. George's" they wish the hosts as much as the singers: 200 cows and 150 bulls each. But they are just as mean to the stingy hosts:

> Neither a farm, nor a courtyard
> Not any chicken feathers!
> May God grant you
> Cockroaches and bed bugs!

The seventh Thursday after Easter was called Semik, and the week

---

The energy of the willow was supposed to be transferred to the person being whipped. On Palm Sunday a willow branch was given to the flocks to eat so that they would be protected for the entire year from illness. The flocks were beaten, while young boys said: "Just as the willow grows, so you will grow!" Ibid.

*E. S. Radčenko, "Selo bužarovo Voskresenskogo rajona Moskovskogo okruga," *Trudy obščestva izučenija moskovskoi oblasti* 3 (1929), p. 126. See also Zemcovskij, p. 27.

in which it occurred was called "green" or *rusalnaja* [water sprite] week.[11] A birch, chosen in the forest for this holiday, was "curled," that is, the ends of its twigs were twisted and knotted in the form of wreaths. The tops of the birches were sometimes bound or bent down toward the earth and tied to the grass; under the birches girls wove wreaths of flowers or birch twigs. Under the tree they performed *xorovods* and sang traditional *xorovod* love songs or special songs which they sang only for Semik and which were therefore called *semickajas*. A custom of kissing through the wreaths was called *kumit'sja*, and it was believed that having kissed through the wreaths, girls became friends for life. They also performed other ritual acts. At the close of the holiday, they threw the wreaths into the water and guessed their own future through this ritual.

The cycle of spring ritual festival ended with the rites for Ivan Kupala [St. John's Eve, June 23][12] coinciding with the summer solstice (contemporary astronomical date, around 22 June). The custom of lighting a fire on this night and jumping through it had been retained. Russian Kupala songs have disappeared, but we know what they were like through indirect sources such as the Belorussian and Ukrainian Kupala songs.

From this day on, singing songs and playing ritual games were curtailed until the harvest. This is certainly understandable: the sole purpose of the rites was to ensure a good harvest; from the moment when the crops germinated and began to grow, the rites were discontinued, since they were no longer necessary. From the day of Ivan Kupala the sun was on the wane.

The songs sung during the gathering of the harvest were no longer of a ritual nature.[13] The beginning of the harvest was called *zažinki* and the end *dožinki*. For the gathering of the harvest peasant families joined together and took turns working on each other's land. Such an organization was called *tolóka* [a work party] or *pomoč'* [help]. Each host was obligated to provide entertainment on the day the others worked for him. The contents of the harvest songs were praises of the host, the hostess, and the one who brought out the cup as well as hope that the work would be finished quickly.

This is the general nature of the calendar ritual agricultural poetry. The number of songs that have been preserved is not great, but the songs have great scholarly and artistic significance.

III

Ritual poetry represents only one side of peasant life. Turning to non-ritual songs, we must first look at the songs about peasant slavery.[14] During the period of serfdom, characterized by feudal landownership, and later during capitalistic oppression, the life of the peasant was extremely difficult; the statistics on peasant revolts show a constant increase in their number and range, so that we might expect the songs

about peasant slavery to be numerous. But the quantity is actually neg-
ligible, and very insignificant in comparison with the enormous number
of songs which compose the basic corpus of the peasant lyric, for example,
love songs, wedding songs, and family songs. How can this be explained?

One of the main reasons is that in the eyes of the peasants the song
collector, even if he sympathized with the people, was a gentleman, that
is, a landowner or an official; and the peasants did not sing the songs
directed against the landowners in the presence of a collector who had
come from the city. In turn, the collectors of the nineteenth century
also knew that such songs were dangerous.

There is another possible reason for the small number of songs about
serfdom. One may have noticed that songs of a very concrete nature do
not remain in existence for a long period of time. For example, historical
songs about the nineteenth-century wars have been almost completely
forgotten. For this reason songs about serfdom might also have been
forgotten after serfdom was abolished.

Nevertheless, these explanations do not fully account for the small
number of such songs. If there had been many songs of this type, we
would have learned of them in spite of any obstacles that may have
existed. The basic reason for the scarcity of these songs apparently lies
in the nature of lyric song itself. As we shall see, a song presents a
poetized version of reality. But not everything lends itself to poetization.
The folk have poetized the battle against the feudal-landowner oppression
in songs about Ermak, Razin, and Pugačëv,[15] that is, in the genre of
historical songs. The constant, daily struggle with the landlord oppressor
did not provide obliging soil for the creation of lyric songs. Nevertheless,
such songs do exist, and they are extremely interesting.

The majority of songs about serfdom express the unendurable conditions in which the enslaved peasantry lived and were most often sung
by women. A housemaid feels like flying like a bird to her mother, telling
her how difficult it is to live in the manor house, and begging to be
ransomed. But there is nothing with which to ransom the daughter, and
the mother urges her to be patient (see #34). Ransom was the only legal
means of escape from the state of serfdom, but this way out was
closed for the majority of peasants; only rich ones sometimes had this
opportunity.

In several variants of the well-known song "Kalinuška s malinuškoi
vodoi zalilo" [The guelder-rose bush and the raspberry bush] a woman
turns into a little bird after three years of marriage and flies home, but
no one is there any longer: her parents have been taken beyond the Volga,
her older brother has been taken to be a soldier, her middle brother to
be a valet, and her younger brother to be a steward (#37).

This song does not contain a call to rebellion or protest. Such protest
appears in much later local songs about the Obozersk village. In "Vy
kudri l', moi kudri" [You curls, oh my curls], an "evil boyar-lord"

destroyed the whole village by continually sending everyone to work. But in this case the peasants "assembled on a steep hill," that is, they held a meeting, organized themselves, and "renounced their boyar-lord" (#35). The song does not tell how this conflict ends.

Some songs portray even sharper conflicts. The song "Kak vo gorode vo Ustjužine" [Once in the City of Ustjužin] describes the "arrival of the execution squad of the white tsar," that is, of a punitive detachment for suppressing the peasants. The whole male population hid in the forest. But in this song as well, the affair does not reach open rebellion. It finishes with a call to send the tsar "a petition from all of them, of one blood, one blood, one tear." The peasants believed in some form of higher justice, even while they knew that the "execution" had been sent by the very "white, orthodox tsar" himself. The contradiction and onesidedness of the peasant psyche in this song are expressed very clearly (#36).

One illusion of the agricultural peasants was that the life of the manor serfs was easier than their own. To serve a lord his coffee or dress him was not considered real work by the peasant used to the hardships of physical labor. But such illusions are dispersed by the songs of the manor serfs. Some songs, in which the content is an argument between the agricultural peasants and the manor serfs, describe the abuses that the manor serfs endured for the slightest offense. The life of a serf was everywhere equally difficult.

The degree of poverty which ravaged serf villages can be witnessed in the song "Gosudar' ty naš, Sidor Karpovič" [Oh, my lord, Sidor Karpovich]. In a seemingly joking, question-and-answer form, this song tells how the seventy-year-old Sidor Karpovich and his seven children, clad in bast sandals, will have to wander through the world in the hard winter frost and live only by begging. Although no mention is made of any landowners, this is perhaps the most sinister portrayal in song of peasant poverty. It is not local, it does not speak about particular land-owners of the Obozersk village or any other one, but of Russia in general, and it is well known in numerous variants (#38).

The song "Kak za barami žit'e bylo privol'noe" [How free life was for the lords] occupies a special position among folk songs about serfdom. The text of this song was drawn by N. L. Brodsky from a court case of the 1840s concerning the escape of serfs from Saratov province and was published in his article "Krepostnoe pravo v narodnoj poezii" [Serfdom in Folk Poetry].* The text was found among the papers of a certain Abutin, who was accused of inciting the peasants to escape. Brodsky says that in the 1840s the song was widely sung among the peasants of

---

*N. L. Brodskij, *Velikaja reforma* [The Great Reform], IV (St. Petersburg, 1911). A revised version of this article was published in the chrestomathies of S. I. Vasilenok and V. M. Sidel'nikov, *Ustnoe poètičeskoe tvorčestvo russkogo naroda* [Oral Poetry of the Russian People] (Moscow, 1954).

Saratov province. In this "clandestine" song the misfortunes of the serfs
as well as their inhumane treatment is discussed openly and with unusually realistic power. The song is put into the mouth of robbers who
"plough," but not a field; who collect bread without sowing; and who
thrash with poles the noble's heads and merchants' backs. The text of
this song has been transcribed among the peasants during the Soviet
period in the Ul'janov region, Menekess district, village of Nikol'skoe.
The ending of this variant differs from Brodsky's:

> We are sending the noble lords off to the ropes
> We are putting the officials and police in dog-collars,
> We are sending factory owners to hang on the birches,
> But the honest peasants we are sending off to freedom.*

IV

The richest area of Russian lyric songs are songs about love and family
life. It is possible to distinguish two types of songs according to the form
in which they are performed. Some can be performed under any conditions: while working or resting, at a *posidelka* or at a *večerinka*,[16] on
the road, in a boat, and by solo voice or by a chorus. They are performed
with voices only, with no accompaniment or any type of body movement
corresponding to the rhythm. No term has been established for them in
the scholarship relating to these songs. In Siberia they are called *progolosnaja* (that is, performed by voices only); however, in other places
largo songs are called *progolosnaja*. In his 1877 collection, Rimsky-Korsakov called them *golosavaja* (from *golos* [voice]).

Other songs are performed during the *xorovods,* during various
games[17] and dances. This distinction is essential, although it is not
always strictly maintained, since from time immemorial *xorovod* songs
have been performed by voice alone as well as accompanied by mime or
other movements. The existence of two basic forms of performance is
quite apparent. These two types of songs are distinguished not only by
their performance, but by their style, their poetic devices, and the mood
expressed in them. Let us first look at the songs performed by voice alone.

There is a widespread opinion that Russian song is melancholy and
thereby expresses the soul of the people, but this is only partly true. To
be sure, the majority of vocal songs, that is, the slow songs, are melancholy, but *xorovods* on the contrary have a humorous character, and
many songs that are not *xorovod* songs are bouyant and joyful. The large
number of melancholy songs of an elegiac character is explained not by

---

*V. M. Sidel'nikov and V. Ju. Krupjanskaja, comp., *Volžskij fol'klor* [Volga Folklore]
(Moscow, 1937), p. 80.

a special cast of the Russian soul but by the way of life of the old Russian patriarchal serf village.

Love songs were composed by young people, and they express a healthy striving for a strong, pure, and constant feeling. If this is achieved, the song is about happy love. These songs contain a declaration of love that is not expressed directly, but allegorically. The love of a young man is reflected, for example, in the way he silently walks up to a girl and helps her with her work. Often there is an invitation to come out for a rendezvous. The conventional sign is a snowball thrown against a wall or window. The sweetheart is called to join the *xorovod* or go for a walk. Gifts play a large role in such love songs, and the most desired gift is a ring. Many of the songs express how nice a girl's sweetheart is; he is better than all the others, just as the young man's beloved is also better than all the rest. In their content these songs resemble the *veličal'naja pesnja* [praise songs]. Several of these songs have a humorous character. The sweetheart is so beautiful that everyone stares at her, even the priest. A pretty girl has many suitors; she is able to choose. But she actually never chooses, rejecting everyone except the one whom she has loved for a long time. Consideration of gain or of a material order play no role; it is impossible to buy love by gifts or promises. She selects the poorest, but the merriest, the one who is dear to her heart. In the same way a young man rejects a princess or a noblewoman and chooses instead "his neighbor's girl," who will be a good wife to him and a "welcomer" to guests.

In these songs the young people themselves seek their fate and find it. But in the patriarchal village the choice was often limited by parental desire. Marriages of convenience were arranged: girls were given to rich old men, or the parents rushed to secure a transaction in which the girls were given to men so young they were still boys. A girl wanted to marry someone her own age, who would be her friend. Until the marriage transaction had been completed, the songs about an old man who is a potential husband are humorous; the songs of the young wives, as we will see, are definitely of quite a different nature.

The songs are more often about unhappy love than about happy love. Unhappy love is caused by obstacles, which may be of an inner nature, reflecting the complexities of mutual relationships; or they may be of an exterior nature, that is, in the power that the elders have over the young and on the whole tenor of the persistent, traditional patriarchal life. Difficult and tragic conflicts ensued.

An unshared feeling leads to songs of an elegiac nature. All possible aspects of unhappy love are expressed in these songs. Very often the songs tell of separation and betrayal. Betrayal is the greatest sorrow, and in a series of beautiful elegiac maiden songs this sorrow is poured out. A girl's tears drop on the snow, and the snow melts at that spot. Spring comes, but nothing holds any joy for the abandoned girl.

Sometimes, however, these songs are not simply elegiac. A girl vows to do away with her unfaithful friend, as well as her rival, and finds the means to carry out this terrible threat.

Love demands fidelity and does not admit betrayal. Songs about jealousy are full of passionate drama. In the struggle of undivided love, lovers do not stop at crimes which lead to prison and penal servitude.

We should not, however, exaggerate the presence of such conflict in song and make any generalizations about these songs. Love did not always end tragically. Love led to marriage, and several songs foresee the happy fulfillment of mutual faith and affection. This is expressed allegorically: the beads of a necklace are strewn about, but no one gathers the beads, neither brothers nor sisters:

> The bold young man
> Gathers, gathers seed pearls
> With the soul of a beautiful maiden.

Another large group of love and family songs are the *xorovod*, game, and various dance songs. Unlike *progolosnaja* or *golosovaja* songs, which are performed vocally only, these songs are accompanied by various body movements of the *xorovod* or by dancing to the rhythm of the melody. They do not make up a single entity because of the different ways they are performed. *Xorovods* and games in the open air are extremely varied. The *xorovod* may be performed by various movements in a circle (usually to the left, according to the sun), with or without stopping; and there can be two circles, one inside, the other outside, moving in opposite directions. While those moving in the circle sing, those standing inside the circle (a young man, or a girl, or a pair) perform or portray what is being sung. Songs accompanying these movements are called *krugovaja* [circlelike] songs. The chorus may form either a circle or a chain; it can perform different movements in a straight line or in various line formations. Such a song is often called a *xodovaja* [walking song]. The folk term for a chorus extended in this way is *ulica* [street], and the songs they perform are sometimes called *uličnaja* songs [street songs]. The players may stand in pairs or move in a chain, along an axis, in columns, or in a spiral, stepping forward and then back. They may perform movements with their hands (clapping), with their feet (stamping), or with the whole body; all this is done in time to the song. The word *xorovod* is not Russian and is often distorted (*korogod*, for example). In a game, the *xorovod* is often called *gorod* [city]. One of the players stands inside or outside the "city" and must find the gate or break through the wall. The form of the game is sometimes established from the song itself. Thus, in the song "Kak vo gorode carevna" [Once in a city the tsarevna], a girl ("the tsarevna") stands "in the middle of the circle," and the young man ("the tsar's son") "strolls outside the city." In the game he must "break through the gates" and kiss the beautiful tsarevna (#51). *Xorovod* songs accompanied by games may be called *xorovod* games.

Dance songs are also included among game and *xorovod* songs, that is, those in which there is dancing while they are performed. Among the folk such songs are also called "častaja" [allegro] songs.

In several provinces, the *xorovod* was "gathered." Passing along the streets, the participants of the *xorovod* being gathered summoned young men and women who were in their houses to come join them, and they called them out with special songs called *nabornaja* or *sbornaja* [gathering songs]. A girl called out a young man, a young man called out a girl, and they would take each other by the arm. In this way a chain was formed that kept growing until they reached the place in the village or beyond it where the *xorovod* was gathering.

Gathering songs appeared mainly in the provinces of Novgorod, Pskov, and Tver, and less often in Archangel and Olonetsk. However, there are reasons to suggest that the songs were more widely distributed, but that collectors did not know about them.

Gathering songs (see #46) always end with a call to join the players. The content is quite varied, but it always refers directly or indirectly to the gathering of the *xorovod* and to the feelings with which the participants enter this *xorovod*. In several of them, as in the love lyrics, a young man or woman is praised or, by contrast, a girl laughs at a lanky, awkward young man but nevertheless summons him to the *xorovod*.

The majority of games lead to the choice of a partner and a kiss. Kissing games may occur outdoors or inside a hut. If the game takes place in a hut, the players are seated and one of them goes up to a young man or woman and gives the chosen one a sign of recognition (for example, by putting a hat on the floor in front of her). The chosen one may or may not accept the sign of recognition, according to the words of the song; but the selection, of course, is finally made and the game ends with a kiss.

Xorovod, game, and dance songs can be divided thematically into love and family songs. Amorous content is expressed not only by the text of the song but also by a game. It is based on the admission that one girl is better than all the others. She is not only chosen in the game but praised in the song. The poetization is composed of the extolment of the one being praised. The beauty of the girl is totally of an earthly nature; her brows, cheeks, face, and braid are described. But at the same time this beauty is transformed, and this transformation is one of the principles of peasant poetics. As in a fairy tale, the hero is often a tsarevich [tsar's son], and the heroine a tsarevna [tsar's daughter]. Just as in the epic song, Mikula Selyaninovich ploughs in a sable coat and green Moroccan boots, in the game-love songs the groom is the tsar's son, and the bride is a tsarevna wearing a shining crown and a gold ring.

One must not think that such lyrical praise predominates in these songs. The depth and beauty of feeling is concealed behind wholesome merry joking and mockery. *Xorovod* games are always cheerful, as in the one about the little rabbit which is found in many localities. Some songs describe how the little rabbit is caught and cannot tear himself away (these actions are also portrayed in the game); in other songs the little rabbit tells of his adventures and of the three maids (one of whom seems nicer than the rest) who greeted, entertained, and then beat him. The participants act out all of this while they sing, and the song is interpreted allegorically.

Among the folk, dance songs are called *častaja* [allegro] songs; they can be performed both solo and in chorus. Collectors do not always designate these songs as dance songs, and an "allegro" song sometimes must be identified by its sharp, clearcut rhythm and sometimes by its couplet structure. It sometimes has a cheerful or nonsensical refrain which serves to emphasize the rhythm; to divide the song into equal rhythmic, musical, and verbal parts; and to create a cheerful mood that will incline people to dance to the music. The exact limits between dance and game songs are not always easily drawn. In many dance songs, youth and beauty are extolled, sometimes with gibes at old age (the habits of the young and old, for example, are portrayed). The song affirms the right to life above all for the young, healthy, and strong. Part of the taunts are directed at monks and nuns, for whom love is forbidden. But even monks yield to the charms of song: the songs tell how they rush into the dance, throwing the signs of their monkish order on the floor. A monk decides to marry; a nun has not really been created for the cell. In these songs the folk reject the authority of the church in favor of the life, desires, and aspirations of youth.

Amorous content also appears in *razbornaja* [dispersal] songs, which are performed in several provinces after the games and dances. They correspond to the songs at the opening of the gathering; just as the gathering songs summon the folk to join in the *xorovod*, the *razbornaja* songs call for the participants to disperse with a parting kiss.

V

During the *xorovod*, and in games, festivals, and *posidelkas* [evening gatherings], couples were chosen, and the courtship led to a wedding. But this is where the tragedy of the younger generation, so typical of the Russian patriarchal village, began. For the older generation, the marriage of a son was mainly an economic transaction, for a female worker entered the household. Her task was also to increase the family, that is, produce new workers:

> The strength should be of a beast,
> The power of a horse. . . .

This was the ideal bride from the elders' point of view. The choice was also determined by considerations of property: rich brides were preferred. The groom was often looking for someone who, above all, could help him in his work. "For our brother *mužik* [peasant], a wife is not an icon but a worker."[18] Several collectors were surprised by the plain taste of grooms in regard to the beauty of their future wives. Because the selection was not always based on love, it is understandable why the songs do not portray a marriage as a happy event. On the contrary, in wedding songs most of the verses express the bride's laments about her miserable fate. It is also understandable why in the songs of married women there often figures a "former love" and motifs of secret rendezvous, parting, and separation.

Nevertheless, the importance of these moments should not be exaggerated. Although the young people could not enter into marriage without the consent and blessing of their parents, the older generation did not always make the selection. If the son found a bride, he was required to ask permission of his father, and if the bride was suitable to his parents, the transaction was carried out. Even in such cases, however, the bride still lamented: it is typical that there are no happy love songs relating to this ritual, only bitter songs about the sad fate of a girl entering another family where no affection awaited her.

Wedding poetry occupies a very significant place in Russian folk lyrics. They are ritual lyrics in the sense that many wedding songs were never performed outside the wedding ritual and, to a certain extent, they have no meaning outside this rite. Therefore, they can be understood and studied only by taking into account the ritual of which they are a part. It would be incorrect to study these songs as "purely" lyric. However, based on their content and character they are so closely related to love and family lyrics that they cannot be studied outside the framework of women's folk lyrics in general.

Wedding poetry is not only rich in material but also extremely diverse in its local variants. Nevertheless, there is definitely a distinctly Russian type of wedding, and this type is what concerns us here. Our study is complicated by the fact that no single folklorist has observed the entire course of the wedding ritual, from the matchmaking through the post-wedding ceremonies. Most witnesses have been present only at the marriage ceremony. Everything else that has been noted down is based on the recollections of local inhabitants. Collectors have had to reconstruct the picture of the ritual for different areas piece by piece, carefully arranging the parts into a whole. One of the most complete, well-ordered, and trustworthy accounts was done by a Yaroslavl peasant, S. Ja. Derunov, who knew the wedding ritual from beginning to end. His transcription goes back to the first quarter of the nineteenth century, and it was published in *Trudy Jaroslavskogo statističeskogo komiteta* [Transactions of the Yaroslavl Statistical Committee], No. 5, 1868. The folklorist P.

Shein reprinted this document with supplementary material but with some omissions in his collection *Velikorus* [Great Russia].

The folk referred to the wedding ceremony as a "game." They said "to play a wedding." The whole ritual represented a single artistic whole from beginning to end. The bride's laments, the girls' choral songs, the praise songs, various lyric songs, mocking songs addressed to the best man and the matchmakers, the *prigovory* [formulaic phrases] of the best man, riddles, and invocations—all were components of wedding poetry.

At one time the significance of the nuptial rite lay in the fact that it legally ratified the agreement. In addition, certain episodes and magical devices were to provide the young people with health, a long, happy life, and healthy progeny.

Gradually both the legal and the magical significance of the ritual were forgotten and disappeared. The ritual turned into a traditional custom. The performance of the ritual was very expensive. Young people sometimes married without the observance of the rite, without any entertainment. The same thing occurred when the young people entered into a marriage without the consent of their parents. Their elopement was called *samoxod* or *samokrutka*. As the village gradually became impoverished, this form of marriage celebration was performed with the silent consent of the parents, since it saved them money.

Matchmaking preceded the celebration of the wedding. The father, brother, godfather or godmother, or matchmaker came to the bride's house and made the appropriate proposal.[19] Usually the arrival was not unexpected. If consent was granted, all the conditions of the marriage transaction were settled. The families agreed on the dowry, on presents, on the date of the wedding, sometimes even on the most petty details, such as the number of guests to be invited. The ritual in the Yaroslavl province characteristically began with the episode called the betrothal [*sgovor*]. In different provinces, the name and sometimes even the content of this event were extremely varied (*sgovorki, slovo, propivanie, smotry,* and others). The fiancé's male relatives arrived from his house carrying bread and salt. The hosts and the arriving guests carried on a special dialogue which expressed allegorically the reason for their coming. For example, the guests called themselves hunters of the prince who had come across the tracks of a marten, and so on. The matchmakers were seated at the table. As a sign that the bride was being given away, the parents of the young people had to drink wine together (*propivanie*). After this they led the bride out to the table and presented her (*smotry*). The bride, sitting at the table or in the corner under the icons, began to lament. The wailing of the bride is one of the richest and artistically complete forms of ancient peasant poetry. The basic motifs of laments on this day consist of a request to her father not to give her away so early. She sometimes compares herself to a green reed, to an unripe berry: the girl was often given away very young, almost an adolescent, and she was afraid of the backbreaking work awaiting her in a strange home. Songs reproaching the father for giving away the daughter, as if she had been a bad worker, are found in many areas. The matchmaking usually did not last a long time. It represented only the beginning of the wedding game and corresponded to the betrothal in the city tradition. Between the ritual of the matchmaking and the day of the wedding the bride did not do any work. Her girlfriends visited her, and these visits were also accompanied by laments.

The next episode of the nuptial ritual in the former Yaroslavl province was called *rukobit'e* [hand-slapping].[20] The word itself reveals that the parents "slap each other's hands," that is, through the ritual they confirm the validity of the nuptial transaction. The ritual culminated in the sharing of a meal by the two families who were becoming related, for according to ancient beliefs, a common table is one of the signs of the community of the family.

The laments of the bride were partly related to yet somewhat different from the laments on the day of the betrothal. At first she begs not to be "given away." The closer the day of separation from her home, the more concrete is the picture of the young woman's future in a strange family. While the laments during the betrothal are directed toward the home she is leaving, the laments from the moment of the betrothal are directed mainly toward the future. These songs are unusually strong, realistic portrayals of the difficult fate of the young Russian peasant woman. Not only strenuous work awaits her, but also the overbearing treatment toward her by her father-in-law, mother-in-law, and other members of the family; she will be completely isolated so that it will be impossible even to show her tears, and she will have to cry behind a column or in her pillow, so no one will see her tears.[21] One particular genre consists of question-and-answer songs between the bride and an aunt or, more generally, between the bride and an older married, experienced woman. In answer to the bride's question of how to behave in her new home, the aunt recalls how she got married and remembers her sorrows, and she teaches the bride how to live in a strange home. These lessons lead to the conclusion that she must forget about her own human dignity; she must humiliate herself and keep silent.

There are songs in which the bride sings that her parents have deceived her by promising riches, but that actually total poverty awaits her in her new home.

Not long before the wedding (several days before or on the night before) *devičnik* was celebrated.[22] *Devičnik* was a joyful celebration, a celebration of youth. The only person remaining sad on this day was the bride. She greeted the guests, her girlfriends, with songs, inviting them to come in, and she entertained them with songs, asking them to a meal. Many songs contrast the maidenly lot of her girlfriends to the sad lot of the bride. For her girlfriends, "on every hair is a little bead," but for the bride, "on every hair is a little tear."

One of the main episodes of *devičnik* was the removal of the bride's festive maiden headdress, called *krásota* [beauty]. P. N. Rybnikov writes: "The main adornment of the 'betrothed princess' is a wide ribbon set with glass beads or pearls called a *volja* [freedom] or *krásota* [beauty]. This ribbon is worn only up to the wedding, and on the eve of the wedding it is solemnly taken off the girl's head; this removal of the *krásota* serves as a sign that the girl has parted with her maidenly lot and has decided to give herself into the charge of a husband."* After the marriage ceremony a woman's headdress, a *kika*, is put on the bride. The songs connected with this event are numerous. For example, the bride walks up and down the hut, forcing her relatives and girlfriends to admire her and the *krasnaja krásota* [lovely *krásota*] she wears. Then she asks her parents to take the *krásota* from her:

> If you will not take it off, father protector,
> Evil strangers will take it off.

But neither father nor mother agree to remove the maiden headdress from their daughter. The youngest brother takes it off, or it is passed on to a sister. Deprived of the *krásota*, the girl begs them to return it to her, to put it on her head again. Sometimes they return the ribbon to her, but after she walks around in it for a while, she finally has to admit that it is no longer her fate to wear the *krásota*. This is one form of this event. The songs connected with it are numerous and varied; for example, the bride sings that she will go out into the forest and hang the *krásota* on a birch. But the birch will be chopped down; and she will put it in a field among the flowers, but the flowers will be mowed. Finally, she will take it to the icon in church so everyone will see that she is wearing the maiden *krásota* with honor. In other songs she gives away her *krásota* to her sister or to the sister of her fiancé, with the admonition to take care of it as a sign of maidenly honor.

On the evening of *devičnik* the fiancé arrived with gifts and treats, and the bride gave his relatives presents made with her own hands, testifying to her skill. There are songs in which the bride gives thanks for the gifts, and others in which she decides not to accept them.

At the conclusion of *devičnik*, the bride and her girlfriends walked around the village and stopped under the windows of her relatives' homes. In her laments she said farewell to them and asked them to forget anything she had ever done to anger them. After the party, especially

---

* *Pesni, sobrannye P. N. Rybnikovym* [Songs Collected by P. N. Rybnikov] III (Moscow, 1910), p. 54.

among prosperous peasants, there was a merry ride accompanied by songs.

The culmination of the nuptial ritual was the day of the wedding. In the morning the bride woke her girlfriends (or they woke her) with songs called "waking-up laments" in the North. In them the bride narrates a terrible dream she had had: it seemed that strange people came and led her out into a forest, and her father's house fell to pieces. She asks for cold water to wash away her tears. In the case in which the bride is awakened by her girlfriends, they remind her that everyone is already awake, and they enumerate the morning labors that have already been done.

On this day (or on the eve, sometimes even on other days) the girl-friends accompanied the bride to the bath house. This time it was not for an ordinary bath, but a special "nuptial" ritual bath to which great significance was attached. The songs accompanying it are numerous and varied. The import of these songs is that in the bath the bride washes away her maidenly beauty.

After the bath the bride was dressed for the wedding. The maiden braid was unplaited so that two braids could be made from it, as was the custom for married women. Her head was decorated with a wreath or the headdress of married women, a *povojnik* or *kika*. The songs accompanying the unplaiting of the maiden's braid were sometimes very poetic. The girlfriends sang in the name of the bride. The bride was dressed in wedding clothes, and in this attire she awaited the arrival of the groom.

The groom arrived with his relatives as well as a group called *poezžane* [groom's suite]. The procession was led by the best man. They performed a series of scenes portraying a struggle with the groom: the gate was closed, everyone began joking, and so on. The whole episode is extremely interesting for ethnography and the history of the forms of the wedding, but these scenes were not accompanied by songs.

At this time the bride was wailing in the front room.[23] In her songs she begs that the stranger not be let in, that the gate be locked tighter, that a doorman and gatekeeper be sent out; she asks her girlfriends to form a wall around her and conceal her. The ritual of hiding the bride was actually carried out in various forms; the groom had to look for her, find her, and try to recognize her among her girlfriends, who were all disguised in the same way. In the songs he is always portrayed as an enemy and a tyrant. The bride appeals to the wind to block the road, and so on. When at last the groom enters, she greets him as a ravager.

The arrival of the groom also met with resistance by the bride's girlfriends, but this resistance was of a joking, cheerful nature. A chorus of girls showered the best man and sometimes even the matchmaker with raillery.

The best man[24] did not enter the house in a simple manner, but with *prigovory* [formulaic phrases]. He began these facetious sayings as soon as he entered the courtyard. The best man was the master of ceremonies of the whole course of the wedding frivolity. He had to have a thorough knowledge of the ritual, and he had to be very witty and resourceful. The formulaic phrases were composed of humorous and sometimes mocking greetings addressed to the hosts and guests: to the parents of the bride and the groom, the girls, young men, and children. The phrases were in the form of rhythmic prose, but they were also known in the form of songs.

The act of being seated at the table was also accompanied by jokes. Places were "sold" by the brother of the bride, and he and the best man had a contest of riddles, whose solution led to the concession of places at the table.

During the wedding feast an enormous variety of songs were sung. The bride invited the groom to sit down closer to her. They thought that this act guaranteed an amicable life in the future. Then while singing songs, the bride went around serving a glass of wine to all those present. This was called "lamenting for a glass of wine." When this reached the groom, he did not accept the wine glass until she bowed down to him at his feet.

During the wedding feast various types of praise song (veličal'naja pesnja) were sung. In contrast to the bridal laments, they have a buoyant, joyful character and are very poetic. Although the wedding ritual has not been celebrated for a long time, praise songs are still sung in many places at wedding feasts. In olden times these songs were sung to the groom, the bride, their parents, and distinguished guests.

We will not linger over the numerous and beautiful songs which were sung at the wedding feast.[25] They are cheerful and vary greatly according to their motifs. In the Yaroslavl region the church wedding could take place before or after the wedding feast. The peasant Derunov writes about this occasion: "In some villages of our region the feasting begins at the bride's father's before the wedding, and this is called devkoi stolujut [to feast the maiden], but in other villages the poezžane [groom's suite] come and take the bride away without a prenuptial feast." In that case, the entertainment occurred after the wedding, the form which predominated in Russia. If the entertainment occurred before the wedding, the best man gave a sign when it was time for the marriage ceremony to begin: he got up and summoned the parents to bless the young people. The bride, with corresponding laments, received the blessing. After the merry feast the festivity again took on a serious and touching character. The songs at the moment of blessing expressed the depth and fullness of the bride's feelings at this solemn and important moment in her life. After this, farewell songs were sung by the bride and her girlfriends. One song was particularly popular and was sung throughout the land: it is about a white swan who was torn from her flock and joined a flock of geese that did not wish to accept her.

After the wedding the young people were led to the groom's home. Here to the accompaniment of songs, they were showered with grain and hops.

On the day after the wedding the young pair gave a feast of their own for their relatives, but this event was no longer accompanied by songs. The relatives in turn invited the young couple to their homes; and with this round of visiting the wedding ritual came to an end.

VI

Family songs, that is, songs of wives and husbands about their life, are directly related to wedding songs. Just as the sad lament of the bride prevailed in wedding lyrics, in family songs lyric complaints about a bitter life predominated. These songs in particular have given Russian songs the reputation for being melancholy and sorrowful. As Pushkin wrote: "Unhappiness in family life is a distinguishing feature in the mores of the Russian people. I am referring to Russian songs: their typical content is either the complaint of a beautiful young woman given in marriage by force, or the reproaches of a young husband to a hateful wife. Our wedding songs are doleful, like a funeral wail" (*Putešestvie iz Moskvy v Peterburg* [Journey from Moscow to Petersburg]). The girl, used to her parents' caresses, to her "mother's comfort" and "daddy's will," enters a large, unfriendly family and is forced to do backbreaking work. What had been lamented in the wedding song in anticipation of the future has now actually occurred.

One of the basic motifs of these songs is the contrast between the wife's own distant home, which she has left, and her husband's home. In her imagination, she flies home like a bird, but at home they do not recognize her, for she has turned into an old woman.

A harsh and unfriendly family, however, was still not the worst misfortune. In some songs the husband defends his wife from his relatives. The greatest misfortune was disharmony between the spouses themselves. A marriage transaction or the agreement of the parents based only on material considerations leads to family tragedy.

One of the hardest things to endure was a discrepancy of age. In the songs a girl always wants to have someone "equal in age," whereas for the sake of material considerations the parents give her either to an old man or to a boy who is not much more than a child. The newlyweds "accepted the law," and, from the point of view of the older people, this acceptance was a matter of social ethics. But the young people did not recognize such an ethic. A forced union with an old, repellent husband, or with an unloved wife for the sake of material advantage, was considered immoral by them. Only marriage for love was considered moral. If there was no love, they felt such despair that death for one of the spouses was the only way out. There are songs in which the wife drowns, burns, poisons or hangs the husband or ties him to a tree in the forest and leaves him there. Several of these songs are colored by malicious humor.

There are also songs in which the husband is not portrayed as a drunkard and is not too old; he even loves his wife, takes care of her, and brings her presents. But she does not love him. The law of blood has been violated, and a hopeless situation is created for one's entire life. Such a situation creates the grounds for songs about jealousy. The loving but unloved husband keeps his wife with him by force and never allows her to go anywhere, but the wife always finds a way to tear herself away and escape to freedom.

In the majority of cases, a girl married to someone she does not love had secretly hoped at some time to marry another, whom she loved. A "former love" is constantly and sometimes touchingly celebrated in song. The memory of a dearly beloved sweetheart is something sacred in the life of an unhappy woman who was married by force. But she is possessed by feelings that are by no means idyllic. Her sweetheart must not woo anyone, he can only woo the damp earth: she intends to be the death of him.

The majority of songs about the family are women's songs. In somewhat different tones the men's songs paint the same drama as do the women's songs. The unloved wife, the hateful wife, is a vicious snake. And nothing can change this, even is she is actually a good wife, "unselfish." And just as a wife has a "former love," so the husband has a "sweetheart" who also invariably pulls him to herself. And for him, as in the woman's songs, the only escape is death, and there are terrible songs in which the husband intends to kill his wife, escape to freedom, and marry his beloved.

There are many songs about unhappy family life, and a comparatively small number about happy family life. From this evidence one must not conclude that marriage in the old pre-reform peasant village was always unhappy. Apparently there are certain laws for selecting what to sing about and what not to. A happy marriage is not poetized in song; the people either do not sing about it or do so rarely. In such songs the wife is affectionate and cheerful, and her father-in-law and mother-in-law dote on her. In those cases when the father-in-law orders the son "to teach" his wife, he replies:

> And why should I beat my wife,
> Why should I break my heart,
> My wife is my home, my wife is my abode, my wife is my joy,
> My wife is my joy and delight
> My wife is my life and my support.

When a son is born to such amicable spouses, they rejoice; when one of the spouses dies, the other laments until his or her own death, and cannot forget the other.

The themes of family *xorovods* and game songs can scarcely be differentiated from those of the vocal songs: that same family life and those same unhappy family relationships are expressed in them. But their tone is completely different. What is expressed in the vocal [*protjažnaja*, largo] songs from the tragic point of view is here expressed from the comic point of view. Tragedy is transformed into merry farce. This is one of the means of overcoming adversity. The tragic hero or tragic heroine of vocal songs instead shake off their grief and come out of the battle victorious. These songs are sung in spring, during the *xorovod* and the amorous revelry connected with it. Individuals did not sing, that is, not the ones who themselves had suffered, but a merry chorus of young men and women sang in their name. Thus, it might turn out that in the first stanza the lyrical "I" is a woman married to an old man, but in the second stanza "I" is a woman married to a young man. "I" in these songs is not a particular person, the singer or songstress, but represents various people in different situations. And if in the *protjažnye* songs about an unfaithful wife, the deceived husband thinks about killing her, then in the humorous *xorovod* songs the merry wife skillfully circumvents the old, jealous but good, slow-witted, and trusting husband, and the song approves of her completely.

In the most joyful tones, songs describe life with a cheerful wife who always sings and dances. It is easy to cure a lazy and negligent wife: to accomplish this one must harness her to a log-laden sleigh. A wife's laziness is not forgiven, and the number of mocking songs about lazy wives is quite extensive. And when a husband brings an expensive gift of a lash to his negligent and spoiled wife, it is perceived quite differently from the husband's lash in the wedding songs. The tragic theme of the old husband is also treated comically in these songs. One song cruelly mocks the old husband; he is promised a bed of bricks and nettles, but to a young husband belong love and carresses; a soft bed is made for him with a silken pillow, and the chorus again shows how one must make the bed for the old husband and for the young one. The contrast of the old husband to the young one is a favorite theme of the *xorovod* songs.

In men's songs the husband's mother-in-law and father-in-law are often ridiculed. The mother-in-law is mocked even when she entertains her son-in-law. When the mother-in-law comes to visit or offers her services, the best thing for the husband to do is simply to drive her away and remain with his wife. The sharpness of the mockery is intensified by a strong dance rhythm, the lively nature of the melody, and the mimed portrayal of what is being sung.

It is obvious that the study of only the *protjažnaja* songs and wedding laments does not offer a complete view of the character of folk lyrics or of the life portrayed in it, just as the study of only the *xorovod* and dance songs provides an incorrect, one-sided view. Only by considering all these songs may one trace a more or less complete picture.

VII

The family *xorovod*, game, and dance songs are all comic. There are also many comical and satirical songs about everyday life that are not connected with the theme of love and family.[26] Many of them are directed against parasitic members in the peasant milieu. Labor was a basic form of life for the peasant; it was the goal and meaning of his life, and failure to perform it was treated very severely. Another object of peasant folk satire is the life of the clergy, insofar as it contradicted the elevated morality which preached temperance and manifested itself in acts incompatible with priestly dignity or monastic vows.

Lazy women are the subject of mockery regardless of family circumstances. The songs about "Dunya—fine spinner," found in numerous variants, provides a particularly vivid portrayal of a fantastically lazy, idle woman who does not know how to, and does not want to, do anything: "Žila-byla Dunja" [Once upon a time there lived Dunya] (#82). Similar songs are sung about women who take a whole week to make up their mind to reap. Slovenly women who neglect their houses and all their housekeeping are also ridiculed. The peasant also would not put up with a delicate woman whose hypersensitivity was so great that a mosquito treading on her tender leg would make her lame for an entire week: "Oj, matuška, ne mogu" [Oh, Mama, I cannot] (#77).

Songs were also composed about unskillful men, for example, the well-known song about two brothers Foma and Erem, who do everything at the wrong time and who both finally drown (#81).

Songs about priests, monks, and nuns mockingly or sometimes even sympathetically tell about the conquering power of love. Youth defends its rights to love against the churchmen's encroachments and, on the other hand, ridicule churchmen who yield to erotic temptations. A girl who is being sent to a convent promises to bring in a cell full of young boys. A disobedient daughter's refusal to take the veil is often encountered in satirical songs as well as in love songs. In *xorovod* songs this conflict is always treated comically. The majority of songs about clergy and monks are dance songs. One example is the song about a nun who does not get up when she is awakened for mass, but jumps up as soon as she is told that a fiddle player has arrived and there will be dancing. She goes to dance, since the whole cell is full of sins anyway: "Ja po kelejke xožu" [Along the cell I walk] (#79).

The song "Čto vo gorode bylo vo Kazani" [It was in the city of Kazan]

(#80) also is sung to a witty dance motif. A young monk goes out for a walk. He is indifferent as he passes by the old ladies, and as he keeps going, he glances at the young women (that is, women recently married), but when he passes by the young girls, he throws his cowl to the ground and decides to marry "a sweet, pretty maid." This song is directed not so much against monks who violate their vows of celibacy as against the vows themselves; that is, it is directed not against the clergy, but against the church, against the preaching of asceticism. In this case the song clearly sympathizes with the young monk who breaks the vow of chastity. On the other hand, songs mercilessly ridicule the monk-drunkard who gets drunk instead of celebrating the church service: "Na gore-to monastyr' stojal" [On a mountain stood a monastery] (#78). The satirical nature of the songs is strengthened by the use of literary turns of speech.

Not only priests but also their wives are targets for satire in song. In several variants, the game song "Skaži, skaži, vorobyšek" [Tell us, tell us, little sparrows] (#83) is constructed on the imitation of the gait and habits of the priests and their wives.

Along with the rich antireligious fairy tale and proverb folklore, folk song shows that the Russian peasantry gradually threw off the chains of the clerical world-view thrust upon them by the church in conjunction with the government.

VIII

A survey of characteristic peasant songs would not be complete if we did not look briefly at children's folklore, implying by this term songs of adults for children (cradle songs, amusing songs) as well as songs composed by the children themselves. Earlier academic scholarship did not consider them worthy of attention: these songs were not included in the seven-volume collection of A. I. Sobolevsky. But many collectors, in particular, P. V. Shein, transcribed and published children's folklore. Although there is comparatively little transcribed material, it shows that children's folklore is remarkable in its own way.

Cradle songs must calm children down. It is assumed that a child going to sleep does not listen very attentively to the words: what is most important is an even, peaceful, and lulling melody. Therefore, cradle songs do not require logical coherence: they are small pictures of the world as the singer thinks it is imagined by the child. Animals do what people normally do: a cat grinds sugar and sews a towel, while the kittens sit on the oven and wait to be fed. Cats are mentioned frequently not only because they are familiar to children but also because cats are sleepy during the day. The custom has been recorded of putting a cat into the cradle so that its drowsiness will be transferred to the child. Among the other animals, pigeons are often mentioned, apparently because of the rhyme "guli—ljuli" [*golub*—pigeon]. There are also songs in which animals (for example, a wolf) are used to frighten children: the wolf will carry them away if they do not go to sleep or if they do not lie down.

In other songs the working life of the family is portrayed simply: the father goes out to fish, the brother to chop wood, and the nurse to wash the swaddling clothes. We can see from this that the child was not rocked by its mother or nurse but probably by one of its sisters. In general, it is apparent that the songs were not always sung by mothers, since they were at work; they were sung by old women or little girls who had been entrusted with watching the child. Finally, there are songs in which the child is promised death; these can be explained only by the fact that in a poor serf village children were not always received with joy, and the death of a child was met with relief: "The Lord has released us." But songs like these might have been performed in imitation by little girl-nurses who did not understand their meaning and supplied the picture of death with comic details. Such songs produce a sinister impression. Although there are many songs about the death of a child, they are exceptions.

Cradle songs as a whole testify to the deepest, most profound love toward a child. Such love, colored not so much by tender and quiet tones as by joyful and comic ones, is attested to by all kinds of comforting songs and songs by which little children are amused when they wake up, stretch, and begin to play with their own hands and fingers. Some of these songs are distinguished by unusual verbal artistry.

Finally, songs and verses composed by the children themselves represent a small encyclopedia of village life and everything that goes on in it. Village children knew life, including its seamy side. Their inclination toward mocking, and toward sharp and unusually expressive witticisms, led to quite unexpected effects; the devices of children's poetry have still not been thoroughly studied, but they deserve the most careful attention. Outwardly these songs are often quite incoherent, but this incoherency is only apparent: children see and portray the world differently from adults; they have their own associations and ideas, which do not coincide with the way adults view this world.

IX

The songs of peasant farmers represent the largest group of lyric folk songs. The peasant was so closely tied to his work on the land that separation from this work caused feelings of the greatest unhappiness and sorrow.

Nevertheless, life in the serf village was so hard that it was sometimes necessary to leave the land for a long time or forever. The songs of peasants torn from the land and from their work on it, who left the village unwillingly or voluntarily and are no longer participating in its life, are strongly differentiated in form even from songs specifically pertaining to the peasants, and they make up a particular division of Russian folk song composition. In this category there are no ritual, love, wedding, or *xorovod* songs. These songs are of a very different nature: barge-hauler songs, soldier songs, robber songs, prison songs, songs about penal servitude and exile, and songs of factory workers.

The first of these songs that we will examine are the *burlak* songs. *Burlaks* did not always break their bond with the village, but were closely tied to it. According to peasant custom, *burlaks* hired themselves out in the summer season for various kinds of trades. Usually such workers were organized into artels.

The river trade was expressed the most vividly in song. The *burlaks* were harnessed to loaded vessels by a strap and pulled them against the current.

Some of the *burlaks'* songs are work songs. The rhythm of the work determines the rhythm of the song, for the work was carried on as the song was sung. This rhythm is not always easily determined by the text, but it is always clear in the melody. Such songs were sung when a cooperative and simultaneous effort was required during particularly heavy work: removing a barge from a shoal, moving great weights, driving in or pulling out piles, and routing out heavy stumps.[31]

The *burlak* work songs not only express the rhythm of work but also present a picture of the difficulty of the *burlak's* labor: both the physical intensity and the conditions in which this work was done. People of great strength and endurance who would not be overstrained physically or morally by such work became *burlaks*. The unbearable conditions of labor portrayed in "Dubinuška" [Oh, cudgel] (#88) transformed the Russian *burlak* into a symbol of the Russian peasant engaged in the drudgery of cheerless, forced, heavy labor. Repin's picture *The Barge Haulers* was perceived in this way.[27]

The text of songs with a refrain of the type "Dubinuška, uxnem" [Oh, cudgel] is not completely clear. What kind of cudgel is being discussed here? Why, in certain variants, is it green? E. V. Gippius convincingly showed that *dubina* has been understood as an "oak."[*] Actually, the word *dub* once designated any leaf-bearing tree. When felling a forest in order to cultivate the land, the peasants did not chop down or saw the trees; they cut through the roots. A cable was fastened to the top of the tree, and the tree was pulled down when the roots had been almost chopped through. This method of felling made it unnecessary to extract the stumps. *Podernem* means "let us pull the rope," and *uxnem* means

---

[*]See commentary by E. V. Gippius to "Ej, uxnem" in M. Balakirev, *Russkie narodnye pesni* [Russian Folk Songs] (Moscow, 1957), pp. 345–347.

"let us knock it down"; the shout "green *dubinuška* itself will go" means that the tree itself will fall down. Clearing a forest to cultivate the land was once very common. Later this song was applied to other types of work demanding a singing crew, and the song was sung without regard to its original meaning.

The unusually beautiful and expressive melody in different variants, the clear-cut slow rhythm, and pictures of heavy labor and way of life of the *burlaks* all made the songs unusually popular. Gorky heard "Dubinuška" on the Volga when he was a child and transcribed several variants of it. The song was popular not only as a representation of the *burlaks'* work and for its remarkable melody; it was also perceived as an expression of protest against the age-old "strap" to which the folk was doomed and was considered revolutionary. In 1865, in a revolutionary mood, the naval officer F. Bogdanov (1838–1866) composed a song beginning "Many songs have I heard in my native land" and used the refrain to "Dubinuška" in his song. A revised version by the poet I. Olxin (1829–1897)[28] was published in 1885 and turned out to be extremely successful. The song caught on everywhere and was sung in student and revolutionary-democratic circles. It became an authentic song of the masses during the Revolution of 1905, when workers, peasants, and progressive intelligentsia throughout the country began to sing it.*

Besides the songs by the *burlaks* themselves, there are also peasant songs about the *burlaks*. To a peasant chained to the land, the *burlak* appeared to be an experienced man who had torn himself away to be free and who earned a lot of money. But bitter reality crushed any kind of idealization: the *burlak* returned as poor as he left. Bondage was everywhere the same. There are farewell songs: the whole family— parents, wife, and children—all accompany the *burlak* to work. In others a young girl awaits the return of her beloved, who "has hired himself out as a *burlak*." Everyone has already returned, but her sweetheart has not, and then, finally, she catches sight of a little boat and recognizes her beloved.

Going off to become a *burlak* can be viewed as a legal attempt to escape poverty by earning money on the side. The songs themselves show to what these attempts led. But for ages the peasantry knew another means of escape from the yoke of serfdom—fleeing—and, as a consequence, a life of robbery.

Robber songs were widely sung among the peasants and the city population.[29] In Russia a robber was a common phenomenon of everyday life.** The chronicles had already shown an awareness of robbery; it

*"D. A. Avtor 'Dubinuški' F. I. Bogdanov" ["D. A. The Author of "Dubinuška" F. I. Bogdanov], *Krasnoflotec* [The Red Fleet], no. 15–16 (1944).
**N. Aristov, *Ob istoričeskom značenii russkix razbojnič'ix pesen* [On the Historical Significance of Russian Robber Songs] (Voronež, 1875).

became more prevalent during the Tatar yoke and subsequently spread again and again after devastating and ravaging wars.

Robber songs are songs of free men. As we will see below, the robber is portrayed in song as a fighter for trampled justice. He never robs the poor, only the rich.

Robber songs are sharply divided into two types. In some the robber is clearly a positive figure. The songs are optimistic and sometimes joyful and humorous. These songs may be called *udalaja* [daring, bold]. In others, idealization gives way to life as it is, to harsh reality. These songs are similar to songs about prison, penal servitude, and exile, and they are related by their performance to *protjažnaja* [largo] songs. The majority of scholars consider the famous song "Vniz po matuške po Volge" [Down along the Mother Volga] (#89) to be a robber song. There is no direct evidence to support this, but the picture of the broad Volga expanses and free sailing along the river corresponds to the background on which the action of many robber songs is portrayed. There is no plot in this song. Young men sail on boats along the broad expanse of the Volga; they put into shore, and a girl comes out to meet them. Usually the song ends at this point. But on the basis of certain details, we can speculate that the oarsmen were not simply out for a sail, but on their way to a robbery. The extensive use of this song in the folk play *Lodka* [The boat] supports this. Here a band of young men riding in a boat sing the song "Down along the Mother Volga" and then pull into shore and rob the rich.

As pointed out previously, in some songs the robber is not simply a man who has managed to free himself from the yoke of serfdom; he is a folk avenger and a fighter for justice that has been violated. In the Volga song "Čto poniže bylo goroda Saratova" [It happened below the city of Saratov] (#90) brave "Volga youths" and "*burlak* rowers" organize an ambush on an island in the Volga. They lie in wait for the Astrakhan governor, who is passing by on a boat, attack him, and kill him. The extent to which this song was topical is attested by earlier variants about the murder of Prince Karamyshev and later variants about the murder of the Princes Repnin, Gagarin, and Golitsyn. The song is full of intense hatred toward gentry-landowner power and expresses the ideology of peasant rebellions.

Other songs are directed against rich village peasants or other rich people. One example is the popular song "Usy," which tells in a joking manner how daring young men go up to a peasant who is "fairly rich":

> He lives on a high hill, off to the side,
> He does not plough wheat, but sells rye
> He takes money and puts it into a money box.

They regale themselves at the home of this peasant and then torture him, find out where his money is hidden, and carry it away.

It has been suggested that the song "Usy" is of Kama origin.* This supposition is probable for the variant from the Kirsha Danilov[30] collection; as a whole the song does not contain anything typical of Kama, but is characteristic of Russia in general. The number of transcriptions is small, but they have been widely distributed. The song is firmly rooted in reality. The nickname and first name Us [usy—mustache] was fairly common in ancient Rus. From the sixteenth to the seventeenth centuries, it was used almost exclusively among the Cossacks. One of Razin's followers had the name Vaska Us. In many songs the word usy has been transformed into a metaphor designating robbers.

Most robber songs are like protjažnye [largo] songs. Some are particularly interesting because they reveal the social origins of robbery, showing how a young peasant becomes a robber. In prison, these songs are sung by "an orphan, a bitter orphan." They are represented as if they were poetic autobiographies of the singer. An orphan endures deprivation and hunger; he runs to the Volga, where light boats "bring him up" and the quick waves "nourish him." Thus he reaches Astrakhan and from there leaves to become a robber (#92).

Historical experience necessarily evoked the vague realization that robbery was not a way out of social inequality and that sooner or later this form of struggle would lead to defeat. Many robber songs end with a prediction of the gallows and the executioner's block, for example, the famous song "Ne šumi, mati zelënaja dubruvuška" [Do not rustle, Mother green oak grove] (#91). This song was used by Pushkin twice: in Dubrovskij (chap. 19)[31] when one of the robbers, sitting on a cannon, sings it (here only the first two stanzas are quoted) and in Kapitanskaja dočka [The captain's daughter],[32] when the whole song is quoted and Pugačëv sings it with his followers. By putting the song into the mouth of the leader of the peasant revolt, Pushkin reveals its deep social significance. Pushkin's text is borrowed from Čulkov's collection.[33] But the description of the singing and of the impression it produced on Pushkin makes one think that he heard this song in an actual performance, probably by a chorus. Subsequently this song was transcribed for solo voice alone.

The prediction of punishment is encountered in other songs as well. In some the punishment is described. Some songs about an imprisoned robber are similar to prison songs.

The hopelessness of employing robbery in the struggle against social injustice is expressed in these songs. However, they are clear testimony to the peasants' freedom-loving aspirations and are so artistic that robber songs are among the most beloved and most popular songs that have been composed.

---

*P. S. Bogoslovskij. "Pesnja ob Usax iz sbornika Kirši Danilova i Kamskaja vol'nica" [A song about Usy from the collection of Kirša Danilov, and the Kama Freemen], Permskij kraevedčeskij sbornik [The Perm Regional Folklore Collection], no. 4 (Perm, 1926).

Soldier songs occupy a particular place because of their content and their poetics. Under the tsarist regime, a soldier bore the whole burden of Russian victories. The soldier composed historical songs as a participant in wars.[34] All military-historical songs from the time of Peter I have been created in a military milieu. These songs have an epic rather than a lyric character. Soldiers also composed an enormous number of lyric songs and songs about their everyday life. From the soldier milieu they passed into the peasant milieu and were here performed and spread along with the peasant lyric songs. These songs have been preserved for a long time, and some very early soldier songs have been transcribed by Soviet folklorists within the last few years, although the way of life the songs describe disappeared a long time ago.

Soldier songs portray the whole range of everyday life of a soldier. At his recruitment,[35] the soldier's sendoff was accompanied by laments. It is impossible to relate them to soldier songs proper—the recruit himself never lamented and could not lament. No matter how hard the soldier's duty, the recruit understood the necessity of the summons. The women lament: mother, sister, wife, and bride. Their laments are based on bitter life experience. The songs not only express complaints but also describe the life of a soldier in detail: the difficulty of servitude, the cruel treatment of people, and the horrors of battle. The women knew about all these from stories told by the soldiers themselves. Today these descriptions are valuable material.

The recruiting lament was first transcribed by Radiščev in 1790.[36] Even at that time he understood that the evil lay not in military service itself or in the draft, but in abuses that occurred during the recruitment, in the sale of recruits for money, and in the complete lack of rights for the peasant, who was not able to take advantage even of the laws that existed. Abuses continued even when recruiting was replaced by conscription.[37] In a number of songs the picture of the draft is drawn in an extremely realistic way. These songs have something in common with songs about serfdom: the levy could not be carried out without an "evil noblewoman" who "handed the peasants over to become soldiers." In order to keep the new soldiers from escaping, they were shackled in irons and then taken away to the city. Soldier songs show that rich peasants in the village were in charge of recruitment, and at the recruitment meeting instead of sending those legally required to go into the army, they sent an only son of a defenseless widow. Nevertheless, no matter how difficult military life was, there would be some who willingly volunteered for service because peasant life seemed harsher than military life.

One song portrays serious family disharmony: not one of the brothers wants to go, but the youngest sacrifices himself. With extreme realism, the song describes a military office, the clerks writing at their desks, heads being shaved, the debauchery of the recruits, and the laments of

the women. But even the women's laments sometimes speak of the
necessity of fulfilling one's duty:

> Serve there, good fellow, with faith and truth,
> Lay down your wild head for us.

One group of songs draws a picture of the hardships of military
service. A soldier always lives by his memories of home. That life, life
in the village, is the actual one he wants to live, and the soldier's life
is involuntary and temporary. The soldier always remembers his wife
and children and longs for them. He imagines his return: he will arrive
gray-haired; the tsar's service, with its frequent campaigns and rare periods of rest, will have aged him. He will fall down to the earth in order
to hear whether his parents are weeping over him and whether his wife
and little children are grieving.

In soldier songs the service and daily military life are drawn in great
detail: cleaning buttons and ammunition; standing motionless for hours
at a time, so that hands and feet swell; drill; guard duty; standing in
formation; cold and heat; short periods of sleep; and for the least
offense—beating, torture, birch rods and sticks, and being made to run
the gauntlet.

And yet, with all this, the soldier is proud of his calling, admires his
troop's formation. He mentally observes the army with the eyes of the
enemy: the Swedish king[38] comes out of his tent in order to look at the
Russian army through a "clear glass":

> What kind of Russian army is this standing in formation,
> In formation it is standing and holding its weapons.

One popular comic song says that the soldiers' grandfathers are their
victories, the soldiers' wives are their loaded weapons, their sisters are
sharp swords, and so on. It is very possible that this song was propagated
from above as a marching song to arouse the soldiers' courage. But this
song fit the mood of the soldiers themselves; it caught on and was
widely sung.

The battle songs of the soldiers are permeated by the same mood. A
soldier was not afraid of a campaign. He knew that perhaps death awaited
him, but he wanted to die having said farewell in the original literal
sense of the word *prostit'sja* [to say farewell; from *prostit'*, to forgive];
that is, having received forgiveness from all he had offended. A battle
is sometimes portrayed in a completely realistic manner, almost natu-
ralistically, sometimes with the use of the ancient folk metaphor for
battle—ploughing and sowing.[39] The earth is ploughed not by ploughs,
but by horses' hooves; it is sown with heads and soaked with blood. It
is depicted in this way in the song about the Battle of Poltava, but it is
also depicted in the same way in soldiers' battle songs regardless of which
particular historical battle. Finally, there are songs about the death of a

soldier. These most often portray death in solitude, under a tree, and, much more rarely, in battle. The theme of death is connected with songs about the return of the soldier. All return except the beloved; he asks his comrades to take his bloodied shirt to his wife so that she can wash it with her tears. Other songs tell about a dying wounded son returning to his mother.

Thus the contradiction between the peasant consciousness and the requirement for military duty is expressed in soldier songs. In the tsarist system the soldier was a slave and captive being, enduring torture from the inhumane way he was treated; and he was truly a hero, standing for the Russian land and laying down his life to defend his people.

In the poetics of soldier songs the traditional devices of peasant lyrics are used, but we can observe principles of a new poetics in them. On the one hand, the soldier, longing for his village, is portrayed as a swan waiting for high water so he can swim in his native element. On the other hand, the songs realistically describe not only the government office, where the clerks sit behind their inkwells, but also the preparation for battle, the attack, the firing of weapons, hand-to-hand combat, and a sea of blood. The great patriotism and profound lyric quality of the soldier songs, along with their high artistic merits, ensured their unusual popularity in the folk milieu.

It is difficult to put the Russian lyric songs of the eighteenth and nineteenth centuries into chronological order; however, it is possible to say with some assurance that the songs of prison, hard labor, and exile are from a comparatively late period. They can be divided into those sung about the prisoners by those close to them and those by the prisoners themselves. Songs about prisoners have similarities to the love lyric and are composed with the traditional devices of this lyric. A girl's sweetheart is in prison, and she grieves over him. In the same way the first thought in songs about peasant slavery is of finding some way of ransoming one's sweetheart. Nothing in the songs is ever said about his guilt or about the crimes of the prisoners. What constitutes a crime to the tsarist authorities is never considered a crime in the eyes of the people. The prisoner is an unfortunate person who is enslaved, and the first impulse is to help him and free him. A girl is ready to give away all her belongings: she takes fantastic golden keys and opens her caskets, but the judges will not take the ransom—"Ax, čto ž ty, moj sizyj golubčik" [Ah, why, my gray dove] (#101). Slavery turns out to be slavery forever. In songs of the prisoners themselves it is sometimes apparent that the reason for ruin was passionate love and some crime connected with it: "Ty zlodeika da zlokomanka" [You evil, malicious, nasty snake] (#102). Nevertheless, the romantic content of prison songs does not determine their character and significance.

The most horrible thing that occurred was not imprisonment somewhere nearby, but exile to distant Siberia for hard labor. The famous Vladijmirka, the road leading to Siberia, was reflected in song: "Oh, my mountains, mountains beyond the Urals. . . ." This is the way one of the songs begins about this road leading to "dark jails" and to hard labor; it is about the road which resounds with shackles and is sown with the crosses of graves. But these calamities cannot break the pride of those condemned.

On Siberian roads, in addition to the shackled convict, one could see the runaway tramp. It was mainly those in prison who sang about tramps, since they represented those who had broken away to freedom. The song "Sedina l' moja, sedinuška" [Gray hair of mine, dear gray hair] (#103) tells of a man who has become old on the Siberian roads, where the most terrible misfortune is solitude, since the tramp fears everyone. But here he finds what he did not find in freedom—*polonjanočka krasna devuška* [a beautiful girl]. *Polonjanočka* here, of course, does not mean a girl who was in Tatar captivity, as in historical songs, but a captive girl who had been in prison and has escaped. This song enjoyed great popularity and has been preserved until now in the village song repertoire.

But the luck of a tramp did not hold out for long. Tramps were tracked down and caught. Many of them had false passports.[40] Such tramps were cruelly punished, and a moan bursts forth in song—a reproach to mother:

> Under which star did you bear me,
> What kind of fortune did you allot me?

Prison swallows people forever; it is portrayed as "dark prison" and "stony"; the young man sits behind a heavy oaken door locked by a strong German lock. The prisoner himself often is portrayed in the form of a bird, usually a falcon, and then the prison is compared to a cage ("Byvalo u sokolika vremečko" [A falcon had a little time], #104). The image of a falcon also alludes to the crimes for which the young man was put into prison. He "killed the geese-swans, black ducks," a clear allusion to robbery. But as we already know from the robber songs, this kind of robber robs only the rich, not the poor. Thus the captured Razin is portrayed as the same falcon in songs about him.

If we concentrate only on the words, at first glance a song does not seem to contain anything revolutionary. There is no summons to stamp out social injustice. Nevertheless, the contrast of freedom and slavery had definite symbolic meaning, as it had in the songs of the *burlaks*. This appeal explains the wide distribution of these songs. Pushkin's "Uznik" [The prisoner],[41] Lermontov's "Otvorite mne temnicu" [Open the prison for me],[42] the song "Solnce vsxodit i zaxodit" [The sun rises and sets] were very popular especially in 1905, and were sung as revolutionary songs. As A. N. Lozanova has correctly noted, in prison songs "freedom is contrasted to slavery and oppression."* The song "Vo zavode

---

*A. N. Lozanova, "Tjurëmnye pesni" [Prison Songs], *Russkoe narodnoe poètičeskoe tvorčestvo* [Russian Folk Poetry], II, bk. 1 (Moscow-Leningrad, 1955), p. 433.

paren' žil" [In a factory there lived a lad] (#116), in which a factory worker goes to prison because "he carried a red banner" along the street, was transcribed in the southern Urals and refers to a later time. His girlfriend leaves with him for penal servitude and does not think of returning home.

There is a sense of direct accusation in the songs which portray in almost naturalistic detail the removal of the prisoner to the place of punishment and the punishment itself, the terrible first and last blows of the executioner Fedka (#105). The song "Vy brodjagi, vy brodjagi" [You tramps, you tramps] describes in detail how the escapees are led through the gauntlet and then, after wet rags are put around them, they are led off to the hospital (#106). Songs about prison, penal servitude, and exile composed by prisoners have a slightly different style from the songs of the peasants on the soil. In his remarkable research about Russian prison and exile, N. M. Jadrincev devotes an entire chapter to gaol poetry, music, and prison compositions.* Much attention has also been given to this question by S. Maksimov, who included a series of song texts in his research about Siberian penal servitude.** The percentage of literacy among the prisoners and convicts was higher than among the population in general. Many literate people composed naive verses, and sometimes fairly good ones, with interesting content. The prisoners' literacy explains why literary turns of speech appear in the songs. Songs of literary origin were in great vogue, such as "Aleksandrovskij central" [The Aleksandrov central prison] (from "Far in the Irkutsk Land," by M. P. Rozengeim) or the famous song "Arestant" [The prisoner] (from "The Night is Quiet, Catch the Moments"), whose words were composed by N. P. Ogarëv,[43] among others.† The tradition of the old peasant lyric was no longer adequate to describe the conditions of Russian life that came about in the struggle for elementary human rights and justice, which were trampled by the dismal system of punishments devised by a frightened government. This situation can be observed to an even greater degree, as we shall see, in the poetry of the workers.

X

The brief survey given above provides some idea of the content of these songs—a content of great historical, social, ethnographic, and general human interest. However, the emotional effect that Russian song produces, even today, is caused not only by its content but also by its great

---

*N. M. Jadrincev, *Russkaja obščina v tiur'me i ssylke* [Russian Society in Prison and Exile] (St. Petersburg, 1872).

**S. Maksimov, *Sibir' i katorga* [Siberia and Penal Servitude] (St. Petersburg, 1871).

†Songs of literary origin have been gathered in the collection *Pesni katorgi i ssylki* [Songs of Penal Servitude and Exile] (Moscow, 1930).

artistic quality—its unusual musical beauty. This aspect cannot be examined here, since such a study requires special musicological interpretation.

A song, however, is a verbal-artistic creation as well as a musical composition. From this point of view it is rich enough to exert an influence not only in musical performance but also in a reading of it. A song possesses a highly developed poetics unique to it, and we will examine this poetics, at least in its general outlines.

A lyric folk song is in verse form, which partially coincides with the tonic system of versification characteristic of Russian literature, although to a certain extent it sharply differs from that system. The tonic system occurs in certain parts of the game, *xorovod*, and dance songs. In these cases, each portion of the musical beat corresponds to one syllable of the verse foot:

> Nakanune, Roždestva
> Sejal repu—ne vzošla,
> Svatal Katju—ne pošla,
> Pereseju, tak vzojdët,
> Peresvataju—pojdët.

In this case we have four-foot trochaic with a truncated last foot. Looking more closely, we see that the first, fourth, and fifth lines have only two beats each, instead of four. This is a typical Russian dance meter to which many dance songs are performed. It has the following pattern:

$$\smile \ \smile \ \underset{}{\acute{\smile}} \ \smile \ \Big| \ \smile \ \smile \ \underset{}{\acute{\smile}} \ \big(\smile\big)$$

Songs such as "Ax vy seni, moi seni" [Oh, you passageways, my passageways], "Xoroša naša derevnja" [Our village is good], and "Kak u Vanjuški žena" [Vanya has a wife] are sung to this meter. Four-foot trochaic with four full beats is also possible; in essence, this is really a different meter which does not have a quick dance character:

> Seju, veju bel lenoček;
> Urodis', moj bel lenoček,
> Tonok, dolog, len lenistyj,
> Len lenistyj, voloknistyj.

Upon closer study, the four-foot trochaic turns out to be very flexible, and it varies according to the number and alternation of accented and unaccented feet.

The three-foot trochaic occurs more rarely:

Žila, býla Dunja
Dunja tonkoprjaxa;
Váli-váli, Dunja,
Dunja tonkoprjaxa.

The melody is not given, but the long pause after each line leads us to assume that the musical meter is duple and that the three feet correspond to four beats. A dance song has a propensity for the four-foot trochee. On occasion we come across other meters as well. The song

Sižu ja, mlada,
Na pečke odna,
Zaplatki plaču
Priplačivaju. . .

as a whole keeps true two-foot amphibrachs until the end. The last unaccented syllable is truncated, and a pause is substituted for it. The scheme for a verse line of this type is:

$$\cup \;\acute{-}\; \cup \;\Big|\; \cup \;\acute{-}\; \big(\cup\big)$$

However, the coincidence of the musical beat and the foot of a verse line is comparatively rare. Usually they do not coincide. The missing syllable is compensated for by a pause or by the lengthening of a vowel, and vice versa: by speeding up the performance, one or more syllables can be inserted into one portion of the musical beat.

An example with the use of pauses is the line "Vó pole berëza stojala," which as a line of verse does not fit any meter (one dactyl plus two amphibrachs). In singing, a clearly expressed six-foot trochaic pattern results. After the third and fifth feet a pause replaces an unstressed syllable designated by two vertical lines:

Vó polé beré//zá stojá//la.

An example of lengthening syllables occurs in the song "Vniz po matuške po Volge" [Down along the Mother Volga]. In reading it, we perceive it as four-foot trochaic, but in singing, it has another meter:

Vniiiz po maaatuškeee po Vól//gé,

that is, it is performed like an eight-foot trochee. We will not quote other examples from dance or game songs, since a more detailed explanation of this question demands musicological research.

"Largo" [protjažnaja] songs present a somewhat different picture. In these songs, the matching of the syllables of a verse foot with the musical beat occurs only accidentally. It must be emphasized that in general there is no single system of versification for Russian folk song. There are several different systems depending upon the genres: dance songs, "largo" songs, laments, and epics each possesses its own characteristic system. The easiest to define is the system of the dance song. The most difficult to define is that of the "largo" songs.

Several theories have attempted to define the character of folk versification, including that of the "largo" song. We will not cite them, nor will we repeat or participate in the polemics.* Apparently the theorists who are closest to the truth are those who proceed not from the text but from the melody. While for game and dance songs the rhythm is the basis of the whole song, in a "largo" song the rhythm is not a decisive factor. Its poetry is determined by the melody, for which a melodic rather than a rhythmic design is typical. This melodic design constitutes the "soul" of the song. A long, drawn-out "largo" melody does not so much illustrate the text as express its very essence, what the word cannot express. It is usually impossible to transcribe such songs using a metronome, although it is possible (sometimes easily and sometimes with great effort) to compress the melody into changing tempos: 4/4, 3/8, 5/8, and so on.

The melody dominates not only the rhythm, which is often irregular, but also the word and the verbal phrase. When a musical phrase does not coincide with a verbal phrase, words or even parts of them can be drawn out; or they can be broken off, and parts of words may be interrupted by mournful exclamations. In the majority of cases, these exclamations, breaks, repetitions, and lengthenings are not transcribed by the collectors; they are noted only in the musical transcription of the song and are usually not even printed. This is how a song looks in its scholarly transcription:

> 1. Èx! da už vy no...
>   Ex, už vy noči, noči moi të...
>   Èx, da už vy tëmnye,
>   Noči tëmnye!
>
> 2. Èx! da vse ja no...
>   Vse-to ya nočuški, mlada, prosi...
>   Èx, da ja prosiživala,
>   Ja prosiživala.
>   —Lopatin and Prokunin, no. 60.

This verbal transcription is not completely accurate. The exclamation "Èx!" sounds as if it were chopped off, but when it is sung, it has an

---

*M. P. Štokmar, *Issledovanija v oblasti russkogo narodnogo stixosloženija* [Studies in Russian Folk Versification] (Moscow, 1952).

anacrusis, is lengthened, and contains an extremely beautiful melodic figure.

In Sobolevsky's collection this song is reprinted as follows:

Èx, da už vy noči, noči, moi tëmnye!
Vse-to ja nočuški, mlada,* ja prosiživala.
—Sobolevsky, vol. 5, no. 357

with the notation, "The second half of the line is repeated"; but this is not true and the statement misrepresents the text.

It is awkward to read an exact transcription of a song; it is impossible, with an inexact one, to sing the song as the folk do. An inexact transcription gives a completely distorted idea of the musical, lyric sound of a song, and of its rhythmic and stanzaic structure. We must add that in a performance with many voices, the *zapevala* [leader] begins the song and indicates the key, tempo, and initial musical figure, after which the chorus enters. This division of roles between the leader and the chorus is often lost in print, even though it is particularly expressive and beautiful.

Although rhyme is not part of the poetic system of the folk song, it is sometimes encountered. The folk song possesses such a rich store of musical resources and means of verbal organization that it does not need rhyme. But when there is no strain involved and it seems natural, singers eagerly adopt it, and there are songs rich with unexpected and skillful rhymes. Among the singers there are masters of rhyme. Such lines as:

Po novoj po rošče
Poexal zjat' k tešče.
. . . "Zdorovo, moj zjátek,
Zdorovo, kasatik"

or

Kak u našix u vorot
Stojal devok xorovod—

may create the impression that the rhyme in folk poetry does not differ essentially from rhyme in literary poems. These selectively chosen lines are not conclusive, however. In literature rhyme plays a double role: consonance caresses the ear, and rhyme at the ends of lines serves to indicate their termination. The use of rhyme is optional within a single poem, but in literature the irregular mixing of rhymed and unrhymed lines is not allowed.

In the folk lyric, rhyme appears only to achieve euphony; it is one

*The word "da" is left out.

of the types of sound parallelism. It may occur at the beginning or in the middle of a line as well as at the end. Its use is completely free.

> Zaigraj, moja volynka,
> Zavaljaj, moja dubinka!

Here the two initial and two last words are rhymed. These cases are characteristic of folk lyrics: the place where the rhyme appears is free.

> Ty podi, moja korovuška, domoj,
> Propadi, moja goluvuška, doloj!

In this case the rhyme appears in the first two words (*podi* and *propadi*), the second two words (*korovuška* and *golovuška*), and the last two words (*domoj* and *doloj*).

It is apparent that a system like this cannot be carried throughout the whole song. The folk take up rhyme when it is convenient, but they never pursue it. This is why rhyme produces the impression of lightness and naturalness in folk lyrics. The rhyming of verbs is considered valid (as it really is from the aspect of mere sound value), just as the rhyming of suffixes and endings is applied very widely and successfully:[44]

> V ponedel'nik mlada žala,
> Vo vtornik vjazala,
> V sredu vozila,
> V četverg molotila,
> V pjatnicu vejala,
> V subbotu merjala,
> V voskresen'e prodala
> I denežki propila.

> Vstan', vstan', vstan' ty sonlivaja,
> Vstan', vstan' ty, dremlivaja!
> Sonlivaja, dremlivaja, neurjadlivaja!

Paired rhymes create a certain parallelism. But the folk created other types of parallelism which give a line symmetry and define its inner rhythm. These are syntactic and stanzic parallelism. In *xorovod* and game songs especially, stanzas are all uniformly constructed and are partially repeated word for word, differing only in the ending. In the well-known song "Vo luzjax, vo luzjax" [In the meadows, in the meadows] a girl sings that she will not marry an old man or a little boy, only someone her own age. There are twenty-three stanzas; in eighteen of them the first line is repeated word for word before the rest of the verse is sung.

In stanzaic parallelism the last stanzas are usually distinguished from the preceding ones in content but coincide with them in syntactic structure. Such syntactic parallelism is possible even outside of the stanzaic analogy. For example:

> Along the forests she walks—
> All the forests bow to her;
> Along the meadows she walks—
> All the meadows turn green beneath her;
> Along the fields she walks—
> All the fields turn beautiful for her.

This type of parallelism occurs very often, particularly when a song or part of it is in dialogue form.

A particular type of syntactical parallelism is epanadiplosis, that is, the use of the last line of a couplet or part of it as the first line of the following couplet:

> I was in the forest, I chopped down a birch,
> A birch, a birch, a birch I chopped down.
> A birch I chopped down, a whisk I bound,
> A whisk, a whisk, a whisk I bound.
> [etc.]

The origin and role of the refrain, which is so characteristic of folk lyrics, is not completely clear. The refrain is more often encountered in *xorovod* songs than in vocal songs. It consists of the repetition of the last words of a line (most often, of every second or third line), and it is usually, although not always, accompanied by exclamations of individual words. Also, individual words can be exclaimed without the repetition of the last words of a line:

> Down along the river, along the river Kazan
> A grey drake swims.
> > *Refrain:*   Oj da ljuli-ljuli
> >   Oj da ljuli-ljuli,
> >   A gray drake swims.

or

> At Katya's, Katya's,
> Yes, at Katerina's
> > *Refrain:*   Guelder rose bush, raspberry bush,
> >   Yes, at Katerina's.

In any case, the refrain sharply divides the song into parts. It slows down the verbal development but provides room for rhythmic and dance performance. The refrain gives the song the structural and rhythmic precision necessary for dancing. The refrain therefore is more characteristic of dance and cheerful songs.

Certain external poetic devices examined above are characteristic of folk songs. In addition, the internal qualities of folk poetry are directly connected with the characteristically lyric quality of these songs.

One of the features of Russian lyric song is that it is created and expressed in very close relationship to the surrounding world of nature and human beings. The gaze of the singer is directed not toward himself, not into the interior of his soul; it is turned to the surrounding world, and only through what the singer sees does he express what he experiences. This explains the principle so often found in folk song, of addressing what surrounds the singer:

> Oh glow, little glow, evening glow!
> Oh valley, little valley, my wide valley!

The word "my" is typical here. It does not express the feeling of possession, but of inner belonging and participation. We perceive it as poetic address to nature. But this address may be directed toward anything that is convenient, to everything that surrounds the singer; for example, to people close to him: "Oh, godparent, my little dove," "Ah, mama, I feel sick," "Remember me, my beloved"; to objects of custom, of everyday life, and of his domicile: "Ah, passageways, my passageways," "What's the matter, little splinter"; to products of his labor: "Rug of mine, rug, sewn with velvet." The address to field plants is essentially similar: "Hemp, hemp, my green hemp." An address to animals often has a hidden symbolic meaning which is revealed only toward the middle of the song: "Duck, little duck, gray duck." Every good collection of original folk songs contains a large number of such conventions. We may note here that the object of address is always characterized by a poetic epithet: a dark night, a wide valley, green hemp, and so on.

Even when there is no direct address, the song begins with the setting in which the hero (usually the performer himself) is placed; "At the roaring spring," "By the river, by the bridge," "At our gate," "In the garden, in the kitchen-garden," "On the River Kljaz'ma," and so on. Similarly: "The path went by the smithy," "The beautiful sun is foggy, foggy."

From the very first lines the poetic art of the song consists of the use of visual images for lyrical purposes. The hero and the world merge into one, and, speaking about himself, the lyric hero usually does not name himself but names what he sees.

An address logically must have a continuation. Most often a question provides it:

> Ah, little night, dark night,
> Dark night, autumn night!
> Why did you frown so, little night?
> There is not a single star in the sky!

In another example:

> Splinter, little birch splinter!
> Why don't you burn brightly, little splinter,

> Don't burn brightly, don't burst into flame?

Another form of the principle of continuity is a request or a suggestion:

> My nightingale, little flying bird,
> Don't sing, don't sing in the early morn at dawn,
> Don't awaken my sweetheart in the tower!

It is characteristic that dialogue does not develop out of this type of an address (although many songs do have a dialogue form). This particularly poetic address—to be more precise, lyric address—is an expression of one's feelings, a call to the surrounding world to be a witness and a participant in these feelings. The address can have another form of continuation. Its purpose can be to portray the setting in which the events in the song will be carried out.

> Valley, you green valley!
> Along you, oh valley, is a wide road,
> A wide road, a rapid river.

The address may also portray the time in which the events occur:

> Oh you nights, my dark nights,
> Dark nights!
> All the nights, all the nights I have sat through,
> I have sat through.

The meaning of the address in this case has been lost. It signifies that the whole outer world is shown through the prism of emotions.

Outwardly this sign of emotion may be absent, and then the beginning of the song is a simple description of the setting:

> Over the lake is a willow,
> Beneath the willow is a stone.
> Sitting on the stone is a maid.
> So bitterly is she crying.

In this case there is no address to the willow; however, this type of beginning is only outwardly and formally distinguished from the beginning of a song that uses a form of address: emotion is expressed through images of the outer world.

The last example is interesting in yet another respect: the protagonist of the song is a weeping girl, and the subject of the song is her sorrow. The song begins not with the girl, however, but with the setting, which is brought closer and closer to us; there is a lake, near the lake is a willow, beneath the willow a stone, and only then is the girl spoken of. These few lines reflect a specific poetic law according to which a folk song does not begin directly with the basic content but leads up to it gradually. Thus a song about the grief of a young girl does not begin with the description of grief, but with a tower standing in the courtyard; in the tower is a chamber, in the chamber a little window, by the window is a girl who looks through the "paned window" or cries by the window.

The examples we have quoted are very short. There are songs, however, in which a chain of images precedes the first mention of the main figure. We should note that in these cases enumeration proceeds from distant to near, and from the general to the personal.* Thus, the subject of one song is a conversation between a mother and son about who is dearer: his wife, his mother-in-law, or his mother. This song begins with an address to the green valley; along the valley flows a river, which is referred to as a road, on the river is a shore, on the shore is a forest, on the sands are three gardens; in the first a nightingale sings, in the second a cuckoo calls, in the third a mother speaks with her son.

This kind of composition might be called the gradual narrowing of images.[45] It is characteristic of beginnings of songs, but the entire song may be filled with such progressions.

Clearly it is impossible to make any judgments about a song's content on the basis of its beginning. One song, for example, begins with the words "Oh, beyond the river are hops," but its content is the complaint of a young wife against her brother who visited for all of one night and then left (Sobolevsky, vol. III, no. 166). Outwardly there seems to be no connection there between the beginning of the song and the rest of it; inwardly, lyrically (but not logically) the connection exists. However, a certain break is possible between the beginning and the continuation of the song. This practice explains why identical first lines are possible in songs that are quite different: "Vdol' po ulice širokoi" [Along the wide street], "Kak u našix u vorot" [At our gate], and so on.

In speaking about the poetics and style of lyric folk song, we should mention one more characteristic. A folk song is never purely lyrical, that is, it never limits itself to the feelings of the protagonists. A Russian lyric folk song always has some degree of plot; that is, it always relates some kind of event or portrays a certain situation. A folk song may always be retold in prose; it is true that in this retelling it loses its artistic character and lyric sense, but the possibility of such a retelling is important in itself. The lyric song is not very clearly delineated from the folk ballad.[46] The situations in the plots of lyric songs are always very simple and related to life, as we can see from the thematic survey

---

*See V. Propp, "Molodoj Dobroljubov ob izučenii narodnoj pesni" [The young Dobroljubov on the Study of Folk Song], *Učënye zapiski Leningradskogo universiteta* [Scholarly Notes of Leningrad University], no. 229 (Leningrad, 1957); B. M. Sokolov, "Ėkskursy v oblast' poètiki russkogo fol'klora" [Excursions into the Poetics of Folklore], *Xudožestvennyj fol'klor* [Artistic Folklore], no. 1 (Moscow, 1926).

above. The conventional portrayal of reality is engendered by real life and reflects it through all the conventions of style.

The observation that a song does not begin with the heroes and their feelings or with the portrayal of the feelings of the singer leads us to another observation, to the awareness of the parallelism between the depiction of nature and man.

The purpose of song is to reveal emotions. But their immediate, direct revelation in a folk lyric was almost impossible, for to do so was contrary to the whole psyche of the Russian peasantry. Young girls were not inclined to pour out their personal feelings, but attempted to conceal them in such a way that they were expressed nevertheless. This corresponds to the basic poetic striving of the lyricist not to express oneself directly, but through images from surrounding nature. By this means a high degree of artistic perfection is achieved.

The use of allegory is one of the basic artistic principles of folk lyrics. There are songs in which the first half presents an extensive image from the realm of nature, the second its application to the life of man. Thus, the first half of the song "Už ty sad moi, sadoček" [Garden of mine, little garden] describes a vineyard which blooms and fades prematurely: it becomes overgrown with roots, its foliage dries up, and the ground is strewn with leaves. The second half reveals the significance of this image: this garden is similar to the prematurely fading love of a spouse. The wife appeals to the husband to live in a friendly and harmonious way. In this manner the picture of a fading garden is contrasted to the picture of a faithful, friendly, and constant love.

The song "Vniz po rečen'ke" [Down along the river] may serve as another example of this kind of stanzaic parallelism. The first stanza describes a drake swimming with a duck. But between them passes the "swift river," that is, a strong current, which separates them. In the second stanza, "another woman" passes between husband and wife. Both stanzas are identical syntactically and even lexically.

More often, however, parallelism is not a principle of composition on which the whole song is built, but is only a particular device, a means of making perceptible inner experiences and emotional attitudes. Moreover, the song never proceeds from the abstract, but from the concrete, from a visual image which in the following line (or images) is revealed and deciphered:

> They bloomed, the flowers bloomed, and faded,
> He loved, the sweetheart loved, then abandoned her.

or

> Why did your ring lose its luster
> Why did you, young maid, grow pale?

The question "Why did you grow pale?" would be simple prose without the preceding line. The phrase "I did not sleep the whole night" would also be prose. But in the song it is related as follows:

> The green grove rustled the whole night long,
> And I, a young girl, did not sleep the whole night long.

Through parallelism, not only is material for emotional perception introduced (the noise of the green grove at night), but a fact of one's personal life is given poetic significance.

In the songs cited above, a visual image is deciphered and applied to the life of the singer,[47] although the explanation of the image may be absent. Both the singer and the listener understand, without any clarification, that the little duck is a married woman, and the drake is her husband. In this case we have a metaphoric image or symbol and pure allegory, the significance of which must be guessed.

Russian folk lyrics are extremely rich in metaphoric images. In several examples quoted from the beginnings of songs, the presence of imagery is quite apparent. Fading flowers refer to fading love; a ring that has lost its luster tells of the betrayal of the beloved; the noise of a grove at night when one cannot sleep foreshadows something horrible; a splinter burning low signifies hope that is being extinguished, and so on. These and many other images of folk song do not require clarification for a peasant acquainted with the whole world of song; thus it makes no difference whether the image is interpreted or not.

In the majority of cases the contemporary reader also understands the meaning of the poetic symbols. If a wedding song tells about a swan that has flown away and has become attached to a flock of geese, it is not necessary to explain that the swan is a bride who was carried away to another family. However, sometimes the symbols are so visually clear and fascinating that they are interesting in themselves, and their meaning is gradually lost. For instance, there is a wedding song in which the groom meets a golden or golden-horned deer in the forest and wants to kill it. The deer begs for mercy and promises to come to the wedding. It does actually appear at the wedding and gladdens all with its appearance (see #62). This song was well known and was enjoyed by many. We can no longer say whether the deer served as a poetic symbol or not.

Another wedding symbol is easier for us to interpret: moving across a river along a thin pole or by a small bridge is one of the favorite and most popular symbols of the transition from maidenhood to marriage.

Metaphoric images represent an identity based on a mark of similarity. Similes also serve the same purpose; however, a simile represents a type of rational resemblance, and in the poetics of lyric folk songs it plays a smaller role than does metaphor. Nevertheless, lyrics, and wedding songs in particular, are quite rich in poetic similes.

The discussion above indicates how fully and truthfully Russian peasant life is reflected in song. Nevertheless, it is premature to conclude that a song is realistic, if we understand by this the portrayal of events as they actually were. A song gives a stylized and poetized portrayal of reality through which the investigator can determine the concrete reality which created these songs. This stylization applies to the heroes as well as to the events that affect them, and also to the portrayal of the whole setting in which the events take place.

As a rule a lyric song does not draw portraits and does not portray people; it communicates its relationship to them. Nevertheless, the portrayal of people comes through; their portrayal is a means of evaluating them.

In love songs an ideal pair is depicted: both are good-looking, and at the same time it appears that beauty is defined by health and the capacity for work. Here is a "good, brave young man"; he has "blond curls," "a white face," and "red cheeks." The beautiful maid is similarly drawn: she is red-cheeked and black-browed. Her brows are like an arc and are compared to sables.

This image, however, does not represent a standard. In love songs not only physical beauty is valued as a sign of health, but also elegance and shapeliness, which seem to portray the inner beauty of a person.

> A young maid went out
> Slender, tall,
> Slender, pale
> Very pretty.

The portrayal of people sometimes recalls the slender and elegant features of the subjects of medieval Russian painting or, later, of the Palekh masters.[48] The heroes of love songs possess a particular grace and lightness:

> We young men were strolling
> Along the silken grass.
> Along the sky blue flowers,
> Beneath us the grass was not crushed,
> The flowers were not broken.

In a wedding lament the bride speaks of herself and her youth:

> Like a young blade of grass I am not fully grown,
> I've not gathered all my strength,
> I'm like an unripe berry.

A young man is portrayed in a similar way in a love song:

> A young man withers for his girl,
> A thin aspen leaf.

The portrayal of landscape in a lyric song is similar to the portrayal of people. The landscape proper is never described, just as people are not directly described. But small, individual remarks and separate strokes are scattered throughout the song, which show how sensitively the singer responds to his own natural environment. Nature, like people, is also poetized.

Small details are written out in the same way as the old masters painted every little flower. The favorite tree is the birch, and it is usually white or curly. The grass is always "silken," flowers are mostly azure. "Azure" signifies "sky-blue," but in folk usage this word took on a wider meaning and signifies the brightness of the color of any flower. How strongly singers felt the beauty of trees is apparent in the following line where a birch is spoken of: "On a hill, you stand in all your beauty." Rivers, sandy shores, hills, meadows, and gardens are often depicted in songs: "Along the green meadow runs a golden stream."

The everyday surroundings in which the events affecting the hero take place are also poetically transformed. We should not believe every word when the song says that a girl is by the fence planting mint, which no one is to trample except her sweetheart; meetings take place in beautiful gardens where pear or apple trees grow. Happy rendezvous occur under them, while unhappy meetings or bitter explanations take place under a bitter aspen.

Similarly the domestic setting is idealized: the house, windows, passageways, benches, towels, and scarves are all represented as beautiful; when a girl wants to entertain her beloved, she is described in this way:

> From chamber to chamber I walked,
> Three golden keys did I carry,
> Three coffers I unlocked.

The striking visual and thus poetizing perception of the world is defined by numerous and varied, extremely vivid epithets.[49] The division of epithets into descriptive and poetic or ornamental is unsuitable for folklore, since all epithets have a poetic significance, even if they are attributive at the same time.

Some of the epithets are subject to the same laws of style as those used in the portrayal of people: epithets lend objects a quality of grace and elegance along with unusual colorfulness; others are applied for the creation of vivid visual images or accurate, concise characterization. All nature radiates with beauty; this is expressed by such epithets as the beautiful day, green meadows, the rising sun, the thawing earth, and scarlet flowers. An epithet characterizes people accurately. A rich man has a sharp-tongued, evil-speaking wife; a young girl is called happy, talented, quick-witted, and generous.

In *xorovod* songs, a young girl refers to herself as lazy and playful. A young man is comely and curly-haired; he is a brave spirit and has frisky legs, powerful shoulders, a brave head. At the same time a young fellow is mocked: he has long, crooked legs. Wedding praise songs are particularly rich in epithets, as are the mocking songs addressed to matchmakers and the best man. Colorful, varied, and extremely appropriate epithets are also used in the description of the setting surrounding the heroes of songs.

It is very difficult to trace the history of the poetic style, since no transcriptions from early centuries exist, and it is almost impossible to trace the evolution within the limits of each decade. Nevertheless, it is possible to note that in the eighteenth century a milieu appeared which provided another way of portraying people. Handsome heroes created by the poetic imagination began to be replaced by heroes dressed in contemporary costumes. After the reforms of Peter I, when Western European fashions and new officers' uniforms appeared, images of young girls and young men elegantly dressed according to city fashions became more and more popular in songs. The means of poetization was now based on these innovations. The portrayal of people in song came close to the portrayal of them in *lubok* pictures.[50] Thus, girls appear with flowers and fans, "with good figures," "natural," "schooled," "well-mannered"; and the young men are depicted wearing hats and gloves and carrying canes, or as soldiers—"majors" who charm the young ladies. This type of portrayal is found even in twentieth-century transcriptions.

XI

Songs composed by the workers have an essentially different character from that of peasant songs. Peasant songs were created over a period of centuries, and they expressed the world-view and the feelings of many millions of the agricultural population. The working proletariat arose with the creation of industrial enterprises, first the textile industry and later heavy industry (the Tula factories have existed since the seventeenth century). Originally the proletariat had few members. The worker came from the peasantry, and the process of replenishing the proletariat from the peasantry continued for a long time. The people who came from the village brought their peasant view of life, their songs, and the stylistic features of the song to the city. This peasant stream in the poetry of the workers can be traced very clearly to approximately the middle of the nineteenth century. But at the same time a hereditary proletariat was created which had little connection with the village. This proletariat composed new songs. The mature proletariat could not rely on traditional peasant folklore to create their works. Azure flowers, swans, birches, and little birds found no place here. Yet there was no other folk tradition on which the new songs could be based. It found its support not in traditional folklore but in Russian poetry, and this process had already begun in the eighteenth century.

The first data we have about the poetry of the workers are from songs of the eighteenth century, which already show one characteristic of the poetic creation of the workers. The peasantry had no knowledge of poetry in our sense of the word and did not create any. They composed only folk songs, nothing else. In the compositions of the proletariat there is no longer a unity of melody and word. They composed poems that may be read aloud or to oneself as well as sung. Many of the poetic works of the proletariat were created by individual literate or semiliterate people. The literary mastery was not always of the highest, and it could not have been any other way. To demand aesthetic perfection from these productions shows a lack of understanding of historical and historical-literary norms.

It is also incorrect to say, as the scholarship of the second half of the nineteenth century did, that the poetry of the workers attests to the demise of folk poetry. Peasant poetry of the nineteenth century *culminated* a tradition of many centuries; the poetry of the workers *began* a new tradition. Peasant poetry of the nineteenth century is the culmination of the development of this poetry; the poetry of the workers of the eighteenth and nineteenth centuries is the first stage of a new tradition, of a new kind of poetry. Skill developed gradually, and, for example, during the 1905 Revolution there were already songs and poems of unusual power coming out of the workers' milieu.

One must keep in mind that the poetry of the workers is composed not only of material created by the workers themselves, but it has absorbed anything that corresponded to its interests and needs. This absorption is particularly evident toward the end of the nineteenth century and during the Revolution of 1905. The proletariat sang works from the classics, poems which responded to their mood: "Uznik" [The prisoner] by Pushkin, "Kolodniki" [Men in the stocks] by Alexey Tolstoy,[51] "Iz-za ostrova na strežen'" [From beyond the island to the deep stream] by Sadovnikov,[52] "Nazovi mne takuju obitel'" [Name me such an abode] by Nekrasov,[53] and many others. We do not consider such works proletarian poetry. We will assign to proletarian poetry not what was performed by the workers but what was *created* by them.

The corpus of proletarian poetry includes works created for the workers by educated revolutionary-professionals who sometimes possessed outstanding poetic talent. The poem "Tkači" [The weavers] by Stripan and Moiseenko, for example, can be put into this category. A large number of so-called hymns—"Internacional" [The International], "Varšavjanka," "Smelo, tovarišči, v nogu" [Boldly, comrades in time]—and the funeral songs—"Zamučen tjažëloj nevolej" [Worn out by heavy slavery], "Vy žertvoju pali" [You fell a victim]—can also be put into this category.

We must relate to proletarian poetry in the narrow sense of the word those works which arose directly within the milieu of the workers, as opposed to those created by individual workers, which were then caught up by the masses and turned into songs. It is not always possible to draw an exact line between the works of the professional poets and poets from the folk, and indeed it is not always necessary. The creative work of the proletariat should be subject to investigation by literary historians as well as by folklorists. Works created by physical laborers incline toward folklore. Works created by educated revolutionaries at a desk tend to become literature or become part of its corpus.

The emergence and distribution of such works has been very clearly delineated above. But something is still unclear; to what degree can such works be relegated to folk creation and folklore? Undoubtedly some signs of a folklore nature are present: these works arise in a milieu occupied by physical labor. The difference between agricultural and factory labor leads to a difference in content, but this is still insufficient to exclude these works from folklore. They also possess marks of oral distribution. In the process of their circulation, variants were created and, finally, their ideological content directly expressed the aspirations of the exploited mass of workers. There is no indication of collective creation typical of traditional folkore (fairy tales, epics) but, even in peasant composition, individual creation is by no means excluded.

For an understanding of workers' poetry, it is necessary to study both the songs created by the workers themselves and the peasants' songs about the workers. Relations between the city and the village were complicated and were expressed very clearly in the workers' poetry.[54] A song from the end of the eighteenth century, transcribed in the Yaroslavl region, one of the centers of the textile industry, is sung in the name of young girls and can be considered characteristic: A young man, having left for the factory, is idealized in the same way as the *burlak* going off to earn some money was once idealized. The factory workers are "bold young men" who organize a *guljan'e*, a mass festival under the open sky near the factory. They are masters of rug weaving, fiddle playing, and letter writing. A young girl cannot be persuaded not to make friends with such young men, as, for example, in "Blizko-blizko gorodočka" [Near, near a little city] (#108).

Later songs depart greatly from this kind of idealization: the girl knows that her beloved is working hard: "Komu volja, komu nevolja" [Whoever has freedom, whoever has none] (#114). In many songs she complains that she has been left and abandoned. In the city it is easy to find love that can be bought; no one will take an abandoned girl in marriage.

All these songs are peasant largo [protjažnaja] songs about love. A new figure has appeared, the factory worker, but the poetics of these songs—their tone, style, and, in part, their content—have remained as before. The songs composed by the workers themselves give a completely different picture.

The earliest workers' songs known to us are those of the Altai miners.[55] From the end of the eighteenth century miners were under the jurisdiction of the Treasury. The mines were under martial law introduced during the reign of Catherine II. The term of service established for a miner of low rank was thirty-five years. In the Altai the need for workers was extremely great, and miners served there permanently, until they were no longer able to work. The workers and their families were attached to the mine. But the work force was not sufficient, and special emissaries recruited workers among the peasants of the state with contracts whose enslaving character was unclear to the illiterate peasants being hired. Juveniles were also hired. The trek to the mine sites, 500 to 1,000 miles long, was accomplished on foot. One of the earliest songs is about working youth—juveniles—taken for seasonal work: "Na razbor nas posylajut" [To sort ore they have sent us] (#109). It describes the long road to Zmeinogorsk and mentions the stops along the way, spending the night, and the work; but the main content of the song is the cruel treatment of the children who every day have to work beyond their endurance. Their only salvation is escape, but the children are flogged and tortured to death for trying to escape:

> They will catch us
> And then harass us
> And overwork us to death.

The shocking picture presented by this song corresponds completely to reality.*

Another song that arose in the Altai, "O se gornye raboty" [Oh, that work in the mines], is very similar in style and content. It consists of simple verses of four-foot iambs in rhymed couplets. This form indicates that it was the creation of a literate person at the end of the eighteenth or the beginning of the nineteenth century; however, it was transcribed in 1865 from a worker, and three variants are known. This suggests that this poem could have been performed as a song. Not all its details are clear, but on the whole the picture is sufficiently delineated. It speaks about smelting the ore, and then about washing the gold and separating the gold ore. The workers live behind bars; at five o'clock they are awakened, the mining tools are distributed, and work begins. The work is carried on by hand; each worker is watched and threatened with reprisal by hand or by "rod." The mood of the workers is depressing: "Our heart pines." The supervision is by officers who themselves do nothing. The workers, however, neither seek nor look for any kind of escape. They are satisfied by singing derisive songs as they pass the houses of the

---

*See V. P. Semevskij, *Rabočie na zolotyx promyslax: Istoričeskoe issledovanie* [Workers in the Gold Mines: Historical Studies], 2 vols. (St. Petersburg, 1898).

bosses. The songs reflect class hatred and the consciousness that the workers are laboring for the enrichment of others:

> Let us strive friend and brother,
> So that Pravdin may be rich.

But the main content of the song concerns everyday life and the mood of the workers. The terrifying details described in this song and its variants are also completely historical. The life and customs of the workers in the Siberian gold mines were even more difficult than depicted in this song.

There is also a small number of songs about miners in the Urals.[56] These preserve the memory of the cruel system occurring in the eighteenth century and later under the Demidovs.[57]

The position of miners in Siberia and in the Urals was different from that of factory workers drawn from the serfs in European Russia. The miners consisted partly of state serfs assigned to the mines. The mine belonged to the owner, along with the lands, the forests, and the people, and the enterprises could not be split up. The people were inseparable from the enterprises and could not be sold by the owners, nor could they leave. The mines in Siberia and the Urals could also hire exiles, migrants, and escapees, and such people could leave the enterprises and change masters.

The position of workers in serfdom in European Russia was different. The peasant belonged to the landowner. He could leave for the factory with the landowners' permission and the permission of the *mir* [the peasant commune], after he paid his quitrent. He was not attached to an enterprise or a factory, as the miners were, but to a landowner, and could change his place of work or return to the village. This relationship explains a significant portion of the early workers' songs.

A peasant coming from the village to the factory still believed in his new master. This is apparent in the song "Vy lesa l', moi lesočki" [You, my forests, little forests], transcribed by Kireevsky[58] in the 1830s (#113). "Factory lads," in a purely peasant manner, lament and turn to their master for help, and he promises everything they want: new parlors, new machines, and good pay. The song ends with these promises, and the workers believe them.

The illusion soon disappeared that it was possible for the peasant in the city factories to earn the money so necessary for his economic welfare. In a series of songs a young fellow is torn between the city and the village. The high nominal wage attracts him to the city, but after paying his quitrent and suffering from the owner's deceit and cheating, nothing remains to pay for the expensive life of the city. In tears, ragged and emaciated, he returns to the village, where he is met with jeers ("Let

semnadcati mal'čiška" [A seventeen-year-old boy] (#110). There are also
songs in which a young man cannot withstand the temptations of the
city, and he ruins himself and his family. According to their form, such
songs retain features of the peasant lyric to some extent, although some
are put into more or less regular verse with rhyme.

The overwhelming majority of songs from the 1860s to the 1890s
describe the difficult life of the workers, the conditions of their labor,
and their way of life. The character of these descriptions is of a critical
nature. The workers not only described the difficult life but sought out
the ones to blame for it. In a characteristically peasant manner the
workers still believed in good and bad masters. With curses and threats,
they ran from one master to another, only gradually becoming convinced
that the situation was the same everywhere—the living conditions,
everyday circumstances, the form of labor and nourishment were unbearable; there were cheating, deceit, and penalties everywhere. With the
consolidation of production, the owner became inaccessible, and those
who were blamed for all the misfortunes were those with whom the
workers had a direct tie, namely, the foreman and assistant foreman,
particularly if they were foreigners—Germans or Englishmen. The workers also hated the engineers. But gradually another idea arose: it was not
people who were guilty but the plant, the machines, and the factory.
The factory mutilated people for the rest of their lives. Curses were flung
at the factory.

The miners' songs of the 1880s reflect this content. The work of the
mines was more difficult than the work of the factory; it was carried
on below ground and was mortally dangerous. The workers drank up
their pay on Saturdays in the taverns, and then everything began over
again.

The dating of these songs is not easy, since the time of their transcription tells us nothing about the period of their origin. Nevertheless,
the general tendency in the development of these songs is clear. Motifs
of the difficult life of the workers were picked up by the populist intelligentsia, who created poems that aroused pity for the harsh lot of the
people. Several of these songs were widely distributed, since the difficult
life of the peasants and workers was truthfully portrayed in them. However, the mood that runs through these songs is different from the gloomy
mood of songs created by the workers themselves. The descriptions of
hard life are a form of protest and a call to battle, and this fighting mood
gradually increased and finally exploded. In the 1880s–1890s, songs are
frequently rousing and full of propaganda. The song "Na Nižnetagil'skom
zavode" [In the Nizhnetagil factory] (#111) is typical. It portrays the appearance of an agitator, an atheist who summons the workers:

> We will achieve justice by ourselves,
> We will not work for gentlemen.

The song ends with a description of the workers' conflict with the Cossacks and the exile of the agitator, shackled, to Baikal. The songs reflect the strikers' movement and describe the conflict with the police. The workers present economic demands that gradually develop into political demands. One of the most powerful songs is the "Factory *Kamarinskaja*,"[59] an attack against the well-known merchant and businessman Savva Morozov.[60] But now not only the owner is guilty, but also industrialists, merchants, and priests, and along with them the tsarist government, which

> Issues many laws
> For the workers very harsh,
> And persecutes them
> Without restraint.

The revolutionary significance of the songs grew. The songs were included in party journals and newspapers, song books, proclamations, and leaflets.* Not one meeting, not one demonstration, not one *maëvka*[61] took place without songs. A song unified scattered people into one collective with one will. The so-called revolutionary hymns, such as the "Marseilles" and its later Russian renditions—"Varšavjanka," "Smelo, tovarišči, v nogu" [Boldly, comrades in time], "The International"—and the funeral hymns "Zamučen tjažëloi nevolej" [Worn out by heavy slavery] and later "Vy žertvoju pali" [You fell a victim]—had great significance in this respect.

This revolutionary poetry is rich and meaningful, and, although it was not created by the workers and cannot be attributed to folklore or folk poetry, it has very close contact with it. But workers' poetry as such has also created works of great power and expressiveness. One example is "Pamjatka soldata" [Memorandum of a soldier], which begins with the words "On the fourth the devil took us" (#117). This way of beginning is found in old campaign and military soldier songs. This song was composed in the name of soldiers who hid in courtyards on Kazan Square in Petersburg during the demonstration of 4 March 1901, and then came out to help the police in their sudden attack on the demonstrators. The picture of the ensuing slaughter provoked strong indignation and resentment. We do not know whether this song was performed by the soldiers, but we have documentary transcriptions to prove that it was performed by the workers.

This song was created on the eve of the Revolution of 1905 and attests to the growth of revolutionary consciousness among the masses. Among the songs of 1905 are a number of soldier songs from the Russo-Japanese

---

*G. Vladimirskij. "Massovaja poèzija i fol'klor na stranicax bol'ševistskoj pečati èpoxi *Zvezdy* i *Pravdy*" [Poetry and Folklore of the Masses in the Pages of the Bol'ševik Press in the Epoch of *Zvezda* and *Pravda*], *Sovietskij fol'klor* [Soviet Folklore].

War and later, when soldiers were forced to shoot workers. "Bratcy, gonjat nas daleko" [Brothers, they are driving us far away] (#118) is a good example of the soldiers' prerevolutionary mood during the Russo-Japanese War.[62] In its struggle against the workers, the government tried to rely on the soldiers, but the soldiers were quickly revolutionized.

It is possible that the song "Shoot, soldier, whom they order" was not created by a simple soldier, but by an author who had some education, but it was caught up by the soldiers. The turmoil aroused by the demand to shoot the workers is expressed with extremely emotional fervor in clearcut rhythms. The poem "From the falling fortresses of Port Arthur," by Shchepkina-Kupernik, became a real folk song not only because it was so popular but because it was subject to folklorization and appeared in numerous variations.

The revolutionary literary production of these years was quite rich, and many of the poems were widely sung. But the majority of them did not lead to the creation of variants; that is, they did not undergo the process of folklorization.

Satirical songs constitute a special type of poetry from 1905. They are quite numerous, but uneven from an artistic point of view. They testify to the intensity of the hatred for the tsar after Bloody Sunday, 9 January 1905.[63] The include the song-parody "Glory, glory to Tsar Nicholas," a parody on the tsarist hymn, and other songs.

The songs of the workers, soldiers, sailors, and peasants relating to the Revolution of 1905 show how the last tsarist illusions had disappeared and how the revolutionary consciousness of the masses was growing stronger.

Editor's Notes to
"The Russian Folk Lyric"

1. I. I. Zemcovskij in his introduction to *Poèzija krest'janskix prazdnikov* [The Poetry of Peasant Festivals] 2d ed., Biblioteka poèta, bol'šaja serija (Leningrad, 1970), p. 7, agrees with Propp that the calendar ritual songs are basically forms of agrarian-magic poetry engendered in ancient Russia when agricultural paganism was prevalent. The songs as well as the festivals themselves fulfilled a magic function: they reflect the attempt of the primitive mind to influence nature. See also E. O. James, *The Beginnings of Religion* (London, n.d.), p. 67: "Upon them [spiritual agencies] man comes to depend more and more for his existence and continuance since by the due observance of the rites of which they are the personification, the seasons are regulated together with such critical events as birth, adolescence, marriage and death. The beneficent and harmful powers of nature have now acquired a conscious will in the form of a spirit, daimon or god controlling fertility and responsive to human entreaty and ritual control, or when animated by malicious intent, capable of being expelled and rendered innoxious."

2. V. Ja. Propp, in *Russkie agrarnye prazdniki* [Russian Agricultural Holidays] (Leningrad, 1963), p. 39, says that *koljadas* were sung three times during Svjatki [Yuletide] (December 24–January 6): on Christmas Eve, New Year's, and Vasilij Day (Jan. 1). The *koljada* group had a leader called the *mexonoša* who carried the *mešok* [bag] in which they put the gifts they collected. Propp suggests that this period was related to influencing the fertility of the crops and the farm animals. *Koljadas* are therefore a form of invocation for a good harvest and for the welfare of the family (p. 54). He says that Russians believed the dead had an influence on the harvest, and therefore it was necessary to honor them just before and during the sowing season (p. 23). Thus, Svjatki began with a memorial dinner to one's ancestors. S. V Maksimov mentions that another form of memorial took place on Christmas. In the middle of their courtyards the peasants kindled a cartload of hay, believing that those who had died at this time would rise from their graves and come to get warm. During the ritual all members of the household stood in a circle in silence, in a mood of prayer (Propp, p. 17). During Svjatki, pastry animals were baked called *kozuly*, which Propp says are related to fertility, since they were often fed to cattle as a magical device to influence the production of offspring (p. 29).

A. N. Afanas'ev, in *Poètičeskie vozzrenija Slavjan o prirode* [The Poetic Attitudes of the Slavs on Nature], III (Moscow, 1865–1869), p. 751, says that Svjatki is a celebration of the rebirth of the creative forces of nature. An unthrashed sheaf would be set up in the icon corner (the front left corner of the house) and would be called "Grandfather." Various customs were practiced which foretold the success of the future harvest. He mentions the custom, at this time of year, of the children walking around the house sowing. They entered a hut and spread the grain with an invocation concerning fertility.

3.   *Dvor* in Old Russian meant "home" as well as "courtyard."

4.   Zemcovskij, (p. 17), points out that many platter songs still present a problem to scholars. Different regions have different solutions to their riddles, and many texts have been transcribed without solutions to the riddles. N. P. Kolpakova, *Russkaja narodnaja bytovaja pesnja* [Russian Folk Songs of Everyday Life] (Moscow-Leningrad, 1962), p. 50, explains some of the symbols used in platter songs. Bread and its equivalents (grain, millet, wheat, rye) symbolize satiety, harvest, material security; gold and its equivalents (silver, pearls, jewels, expensive fur and cloth) symbolize luxury and wealth; all actions portrayed as done jointly (working, eating, drinking, standing or sitting together) symbolize happy love and marriage. The majority of the symbols are devoted to love and marriage. These songs are short mainly because of the manner in which they are performed, one song quickly following another in the process of ritual fortunetelling.

Alexander Sergeevič Pushkin's great novel in verse, *Eugene Onegin* (1822–1830), a parody on the Byronic hero and the Sentimental heroine, includes a platter song. The heroine, Tat'jana, develops from a shy, provincial maid nourished on Sentimental novels into a mature, profound young woman of St. Petersburg society. In chapter 5 she has fallen in love with Eugene and uses the platter-song ritual to find out her future with him:

> Tatyana curiously gazes
> At the prophetic waxen mold,
> All eager in its wondrous mazes
> A wondrous future to behold.
> Then from the basin someone dredges,
> Ring after ring, the players' pledges,
> And comes her ringlet, they rehearse
> The immemorial little verse:
> "There all the serfs are wealthy yeomen,
> They shovel silver with a spade;
> To whom we sing, he shall be made
> Famous and rich!" But for ill omen

They take this plaintive ditty's voice;
Koshurka [a kitten] is the maiden's choice.

(Alexander Pushkin, *Eugene Onegin*, trans. Walter Arndt
[New York, 1963], p. 118.)

Christmas folk rituals also appear in Leo Tolstoy's *War and Peace*,
Bk. VII, xii, when Nataša and Sonja use looking glasses to tell the future.

An ethnographic study of a Russian village (*The Village of Viriatino*,
ed. P. I. Kušner, trans. Sula Benet [New York, 1970], p. 135), describes some
of the fortunetelling that took place in the village from Christmas until
New Year's: "Before Christmas they would melt wax and after it cooled,
observe the resulting shapes very carefully. If they were in the form of
rings, it was a sign that the girls would be married, if they resembled a
coffin, that they would die, etc. Some girls went into the steam baths
at the New Year and looked into a mirror. This divination was considered
very frightening and not many had the courage to try it as one was
supposed to see the face of one's future husband in the mirror."

5.   The term *maslenica* is related to the word *maslo* (butter). The
holiday corresponds to the Carnival of western Europe. In his book on
Russian agrarian holidays (p. 70), Propp mentions that in some places
the role of Maslenica was played by a living person. A drunken peasant
with wine and pastry sat on a wheel resting on a pole in a sledge. He
was dressed in a costume sewn with bells or in a woman's dress, his
face smeared with soot. As many people as possible accompanied him
in sledges, and a crowd followed this procession with laughter, dancing,
and songs. In an article on these agricultural festivals, Propp notes that
while the effigy for the whole village was destroyed on the fields planted
for winter crops, Carnival dolls for individual families were torn to pieces
and thrown into the yard for the livestock, which was supposed to ensure
the fertility of animals. Propp also points out that the Maslenica doll
was said to have an influence on human fertility (See Propp, "The Historical Bases of Some Russian Religious Festivals," *Introduction to Soviet
Ethnography*, ed. S. and E. Dunn, II [Berkeley, 1974], p. 377).

6.   In his book on the agricultural holidays (p. 30), Propp quotes
V. V. Selivanov's description in 1902 of one of these spring rituals; "On
Ascension they bake larks. After resting after supper, the men, women,
and children all go out with these larks into their rye field. There each
in his cornfield, after offering prayers to all four sides of the field, throws
the lark into the air, saying: 'So that my rye may grow high.' After this
they ate the pastry larks."

Y. M. Sokolov, in *Russian Folklore*, trans. C. R. Smith (New York,
1950), p. 191, says that at this time the girls in the village customarily
imitated the springtime songs of birds. They sang songs at opposite ends
of the village, one chorus answering the other. When one finished,

another began in the distance, and this went on from village to village. Often the girls held branches of trees with images of birds made of cloth and sang, "Larks, larks, come flying to us, bring the beautiful spring." This representation of birds was thought to evoke their flight and, thus, the coming of spring. Sokolov mentions another custom connected with the welcoming of spring, in which women went out of the village to a field and spread a white linen cloth on the meadow, placed bread on it, and gave the invocation: "This is for you, Mother Spring" (p. 192).

W. R. Ralston in *The Songs of the Russian People* (London, 1872), p. 213, mentions other rites connected with the beginning of spring. In one of them, on March 9, peasants often made clay images of larks, smeared them with honey, and put tinsel on their heads. They carried them around the village singing songs to spring.

7.   Pushkin wrote an imitation of the spring songs in 1828:

> The cold winds still blow
> And sweep across the morning frost,
> Just now early flowers have appeared
> On a thawed patch of springtime;
> As if from a marvelous waxen kingdom,
> From a fragrant honey cell
> Out flew the first bee,
> Flew along the early flowers
> To find out about beautiful spring,
> Whether the dear guest would come soon,
> Whether the meadows would be green soon,
> Whether on the curly birch soon
> Sticky leaves would blossom,
> Whether the fragrant cherry tree would blossom.

8.   In 1823, Pushkin was still in exile in the south of Russia, and his poem "The Bird" uses the folk custom of letting the birds out of their cages to reflect his own desire for freedom.

> In a strange land I piously observe
> A native custom of yore:
> I let out a little bird to freedom
> On the holy festival of spring.
>
> I can now be consoled;
> Why should I murmur to God,
> When at least to one creature
> I was able to give the gift of freedom!

9.   Ralston mentions a rite connected with *Krasnaja gorka* ("red hillock" or "beautiful hillock," since *krasnyi* meant "beautiful" in Old

Russian and "red" in modern Russian). A woman, the lead singer, holding a round loaf and a red egg, both emblems of the sun, turned her face to the East and sang one of the vernal songs, which the chorus then took up. In many places this is followed by the destruction of the figure of Death of winter (p. 221).

10. Mili Balakirev (1837–1910) was one of the Mighty Five, a group of composers interested in incorporating Russia's history and folklore into their music. Balakirev published his collection of Russian folk songs in 1866; *Russia*, a tone poem, is based on three folk tunes from this collection. *Islamey*, a piano piece, is based on themes from Armenia and the Caucasus. N. A. Rimsky-Korsakov (1844–1908), another member of the Mighty Five, published his collection of folk songs in 1875 and 1877. His opera, *The Snow Maiden* (1880), and *Sadko* (1869, 1891), a tone poem, are based on Russian folklore. His opera *May Night* (1878), based on a story by Nikolas Gogol, uses folk song material, including pagan sun worship and games and ceremonies from Russian peasant life.

P. I. Tchaikovsky (1840–1893), unlike the Mighty Five, showed more interest in Western models than in Russian folk music. His second symphony, the *Little Russian Symphony*, however, uses Russian folk themes. In the first part of his opera *Eugene Onegin* (1877) he uses Russian folk songs, and his comic opera *Vakula the Smith* (1874, 1885) includes a number of Ukrainian folk songs.

Sergej Taneev (1856–1915) is best known for his two-volume work on theoretical counterpoint, *Imitative Counterpoint in Strict Style*. He wrote several symphonies, an opera, *Orestes*, and a cantata, *John of Damascus.*

Alexander Kastal'skij (1856–1926) was one of the important modern authorities on folk song and the Orthodox church chant.

Russian folk songs are often polyrhythmic and use scales that are not part of the Western musical tradition. Richard Leonard in *A History of Russian Music* (London, 1956), p. 200, mentions that A. Ju. Palčikov began a new attitude toward the transcription of folk songs, believing that they should not be changed to Western harmonizations or arrangements. An example of the polyrhythmic aspect of Russian folk song can be seen in the first few measures of "Priplakivan'e pered banej" (Lament before the bath), one of the songs included in wedding ritual:

11. Sokolov (p. 193), mentions that during this period peasants used to decorate their houses with green branches of birch trees. They believed that the souls of deceased relatives lived in these trees. On the Wednesday of Semik week the girls chose and marked the birches, and on Thursday, bringing fried eggs and beer, they decorated the chosen trees with ribbons and flowers. After all the birches had been decorated, they placed the fried eggs around one birch and sang appropriate songs. Then, as Propp

U к(ы)_ра_с(ы)_на,   кра_с(ы)_на да у   кры_ле_ч(и)_ка...а да

у   ча_с(ы) _ тых,   ме_л(ы)_ких да   у   при_

_сту_по_чёк...а да   пе _ ре_с(ы) _ ту _ пи_ м(ы) _ те,на_

_ши   хо _ ро_ши_я.. а   да   на   но_

This song appears in D. M. Balašov, Ju. E. Krasovskaja, *Russkie svadebnye pesni* [Russian Wedding Songs] (Leningrad, 1969), p. 53.

describes, the *kumit'sja* ceremony took place. The girls kissed each other through the garland on the birch tree and gave one another an oath of friendship.

Ralston (p. 233), describes another custom connected with this holiday. In some villages peasants went to the forest and cut down a young birch, dressed it in women's clothing or decorated it with colored ribbons. They then had a feast, and finally carried the birch back to the village and set it up in one of the houses, where it remained as an honored guest until Sunday, Trinity Day. On that day they took the birch to a stream, flung it into the water, and threw Semik wreaths after it. Afanas'ev (III, p. 707) notes that the wreath was a symbol of love and marriage and that the holiday devoted to it must be considered the best time of year for guessing one's future family happiness. After the *xorovod* the girls threw their wreaths into the water; if it sank, it was a sign of death, widowhood, or sterility; if it circled in one spot, it meant misfortune; if it floated, it foretold a happy marriage and long life. Ralston mentions that on the banks of the river Meč near Tula there is a circle of stones which are supposed to be girls who formed a *xorovod* on this spot on Trinity Day and danced so furiously that they turned into stones (p. 238).

Zemcovskij (p. 36) discusses other rituals connected with this holiday. In the Vasilij district of Nižegorod province on Semik, peasants make an effigy of a man in a red shirt and wide velveteen trousers and a woman in a sarafan. In the morning, with songs and dances, they take the figures to a field, put them under a tree, and put wine and refreshments next to them. The participants continue singing while sitting around the effigies, then dance in a circle, kiss the dolls and each other. After drinking and eating, they again form a circle, raise a lament, dance furiously around the birch and weave wreaths out of its branches. Every participant marks his wreath, puts it around the effigy, and then goes home. The next day everybody again collects around the effigies and kisses them. Then they destroy the effigies, take the wreaths and put them on their heads, walk to a pond or river, singing the whole time, and throw the wreaths in the water, telling fortunes in the manner described above. The significance of all these rites is an attempt to ensure the harvest.

Propp (*Russian Agricultural Holidays*) suggests that since the birch was one of the first trees to bloom in the spring, it was considered an embodiment of forces of growth. Sometimes, after the birch was decorated, the peasants threw it into a rye field, so that the strength inside the birch would be transferred to the field (p. 75). Sometimes the girls tied the top of the birch to the grass, so that the strength inside the birch would be transmitted to the earth (p. 61). The girls also performed a memorial ceremony on Trinity Sunday on the graves of their parents, and afterward they divided eggs among the family (p. 19).

Semik occurs during Mermaid Week. Mermaids were considered embodiments of water and were believed to climb out of the water on Semik and live on land until late autumn. They passed from the forests to the fields and thus, as Propp suggests, provide the earth with necessary moisture and helped the growth of grain (*Russian Agricultural Holidays*, p. 78). Propp quotes S. V. Maksimov's description of this folk belief: "At night in the moonlight . . . they swing in the branches, cry out to each other, dance merry *xorovods* with songs and games. Wherever they run and frolic, there the grain will be abundant" (p. 78). Zemcovskij (p. 38) also notes that they bury "mermaids" on this holiday. They put the mermaid in the form of a doll into a coffin and take her to the shore of a river. The girls disguise themselves as sextons, make a censer out of an eggshell and candles out of the stem of hemp. At the river they take their farewell of the mermaid, while some cry and others laugh. They throw the coffin into the water and return with songs. Afanas'ev (III, p. 149) says that during this week the peasants made a pilgrimage to sown fields, where they adorned an image with branches and greenery. This usually occurred on Whit Monday, and while the clergy made the rounds of the fields, women accompanied them singing ritual songs requesting good weather and an abundance of the fruits of the earth. He also notes (II, p. 240) that mermaids were believed to be the souls of unbaptized children, as well as those who drowned or were strangled and women who had committed suicide. During Mermaid Week the relatives go to the graves of these unfortunate souls, break red eggs on the graves, and summon the mermaids. They also put bliny (round pancakes) on the graves as a sacrifice to the mermaids.

With Sir James Frazer in mind, Propp argues (p. 95) that the various holidays on which they destroyed or buried an effigy cannot be considered part of a death and resurrection cult, since the gods were resurrected only in the form of vegetation. The Maslenica doll, the Trinity birch, the mermaid doll, were not deities, and there was no cult or temple devoted to them. They appeared on only one day of the year, and represented vegetative forces. Even what appears to be a cult of trees is really a cult of the vegetative force itself embodied in the trees, a force that can be transferred from it to the earth.

12.   The term "Kupala" comes from the word *Kupat'* [to bathe]. The worship of water and belief in its mystic powers were elements of the cult of Kupala. G. Alexinsky, in "Slavonic Mythology," *New Larousse Encyclopedia of Mythology* (London, 1968), p. 296, says the during the Kupala festival peasants bathed themselves in the dew which was gathered during the night of the festival. Zemcovskij (p. 40) says the peasants made an effigy on this night, led a *xorovod* around it, then put it in their arms and jumped through a bonfire with it. On this night, according to folk belief, demons and witches appeared, and many songs are spells to banish these spirits from the barns and the fields.

One of Nikolas Gogol's early stories, "Saint John's Eve," is based on one of the rituals connected with this night, the search for sacred and magic herbs and flowers. The main plant of this night was the fern, which, as Propp points out (p. 62), the folk believed blossomed for one moment on Kupala's night. Whoever plucked it was granted the ability to see a great treasure, but since the treasure was guarded by evil spirits who were particularly active on this night, it was very difficult to get the treasure from them. Since the grasses were considered to have supernatural powers on this festival, the peasants believed they had to be picked with an incantation which only the initiated knew, otherwise the powers of the herbs would be impotent. An epistle from Pamfil, abbot of the Eleazarov Monastery (early sixteenth century), describes it in this way: "Barely had the great holiday of the birthday of the Precursor begun, than the witches and sorcerers, male and female, came out and roamed the meadows and swamps, the deserts and groves, looking for deadly grasses and poisonous substances for the ruin of men and cattle, as well as for marvelous roots they would dig out which aroused their men's passions" (Propp, *Russian Agricultural Rituals*, p. 63). However, any peasant could gather the herbs the morning of Ivan Kupala Day and bring them to church, where they would be sanctified. They were then kept all year and used as medicine and protection against witchcraft, as well as for prophesying the future. The grasses gathered on this festival were put at the head of the bed, and every dream dreamt that night was considered prophetic.

Zemcovskij (p. 41), says that many ballads written for this night are about the Ivan and Mary (*Ivan-da-mar'ja*) flower (*melampyrum nemo-rosum*). The peasants wove this flower into wreaths, brought it home, collected it for medicinal cures, and so on. Poetic ballads that have become a part of Kupala folklore tell of how a brother and sister met and married, not recognizing each other and how, for this sin, this incestuous marriage, they were turned into flowers consisting of two colors, blue and yellow. Afanas'ev (II, p. 471) describes the events that took place on Bald Mountain, where the witches and demons gathered on this night. Each witch appears at the festivities with her lover-devil. The leader of the demonic forces was Satan himself in the form of goat with a black human face, solemnly sitting on a tall chair or on a large stone slab in the midst of the meeting. All those present show their obedience to him by kneeling before him. Satan then turns to the one who will play the leading role in the festivities, their queen. The spirits report what evil deeds they have accomplished during the year and discuss future plots. Then, to the accompaniment of torch light taken from a flame burning between the horns of the great goat, they proceed to the feast and devour horse meat and other viands without bread and salt, drink beverages prepared from cows' hooves and horses' skulls. After finishing the meal, the witches and demons begin dances accompanied by music played with a cat's tail for a bow and horse's skull for a fiddle. After this wild dance, they burn the large goat and distribute his ashes among the participants, who, with the help of these ashes, may bring various types of misfortune to people. The event finishes with a carnal orgy and the fires are then extinguished and each flies back home on a broom. Modest Musorgskij (1839–1881) wrote a famous tone poem based on this Russian festival, *A Night on Bald Mountain* (1867). Sir James Frazer, in his chapter on fire-festivals of Europe, states that many cultures, including Russia's, are similar in their celebration of the summer solstice, when the power of the sun seems to be waning.

Propp, in his article on the agricultural rituals (p. 389), notes that the Kupala fires are not only connected with purification (jumping through it is supposed to preserve health and cure disease), but is also supposed to embody a creative life force which is transferred to those who jump through it.

13.   In his book, Propp (p. 65) notes that the first sheaf of the harvest was not put into the haystack, but was solemnly brought into the house, put into a corner or under an icon, and decorated with wreaths of flowers or ears of corn. The kernels from it were brought to church to be blessed, and then mixed with the seeds to be used to sow the fields. The peasants thought that the first sheaf contained great strength, that its seeds would influence the bountiful growth of the next crop. At the end of the harvest a patch of corn was left unmown, called *boroda* [beard.] The original sense of the word has been lost. Sometimes they wove these ears together,

and said, "Well, Il'ja-beard, for summer bear us rye and oats!" The last
sheaf was decorated with ribbons and flowers, sometimes dressed in
peasant woman's clothes, and to the accompaniment of singing it was
carried into the house. Propp interprets this ritual as a means of bringing
health and prosperity to the home. The kernels of this sheaf were also
mixed with seeds that were later used for sowing, and in some areas the
last sheaf was fed to the cattle, presumably to aid their productivity. In
summarizing all these rituals, Propp says (p. 66), "All this shows that
the strength coming out of the earth into the ears of corn is passed
through them back to the earth." Frazer, in *The New Golden Bough*, ed.
T. H. Gaster (New York, 1964), pp. 516–518, describes the custom of plaiting
corn in various parts of England, which bears a resemblance to the
Russian custom. Zemcovskij (p. 44) mentions other rituals connected
with the harvest: On the night when the reaping was finished, the peasants rolled along the field with incantations, to return strength to the
field. Having finished the harvest, all the harvesters threw themselves
on their backs, rolled about, and turned somersaults so that the next
year their backs would not ache and it would be easier to harvest. Frazer,
in his section "Sex and Vegetation" (pp. 125–129), shows that rolling in
the field or even sexual intercourse in the fields after harvest is believed
by many peasant cultures to stimulate the growth of crops.

14.   In the fourteenth century the serfs still had a limited amount
of freedom. Provided they had paid the *barščina* or corvée, payment of
a certain number of days of labor to the landowner, or the *obrok*, quitrent,
payment to the landowner in kind or money, the peasants were allowed
to leave their master on St. George's Day in late autumn. However, as
Nicholas Riasanovsky points out (*A History of Russia*, 2d ed. [New York,
1969], p. 175), with the Edict of 1649 serfdom was fully established in the
Muscovite state. It eliminated any statute of limitations for fugitives,
and, with their obligations undefined, the serfs were at the mercy of
landlords, who began to exercise increasing judicial and police authority
on their estates, and the serfs were treated like slaves. The serfs were
not emancipated until March 3, 1861. This reform, however, was far from
satisfactory. Land in most areas was transferred to peasant communes
(*mir*) rather than to individual peasants, and the individual peasant
become subject to the will of the commune. Riasanovsky point out that
(p. 415) "the commune tended to perpetuate backwardness, stagnation,
and overpopulation in the coutryside precisely when Russian agriculture
drastically needed improvement and modernization."

15.   Ermak is the pseudonym for Vasilij Alenin, who led successful
expeditions into Siberia in the sixteenth century and inspired the Russians to push their frontiers to the Pacific. Philip Longworth in *The*

Cossacks (New York, 1970), p. 48, describes how Ermak entered the service of a powerful merchant family, the Stroganovs, who had received a charter in 1575 from Ivan the Terrible allowing them to wage war on Kuchum, the Khan of the Siberian Tartars, and to exploit these lands tax-free for twenty years. In 1581, Ermak and a small army began their advance across Siberia. Although Ermak died in the attempt, he damaged the Siberian Khanate beyond repair, and the tsar was inspired to build an empire in the East. Two years after Ermak's death, the remaining opposition was crushed and the tsar established rule over western Siberia. This land provided a means of escape for a while for runaway serfs, until the government clamped down.

Stenka Razin led a rebellion in 1670–1671 during the reign of Tsar Alexis. Razin was a commander of a band of Don Cossacks who raided Persia and other areas along the Caspian and the lower Volga. In 1670 he moved up the Volga and issued proclamations urging the peasants to turn against their masters and promising them freedom. While members of the upper classes were massacred, soldiers, common people, and native tribes welcomed Razin. As Riasanovsky notes, (p. 195), however, the poor organization and discipline of the rebel army gave the victory to the regular Muscovite troops. Although Razin escaped, in 1671 he was seized by Cossack authorities and handed over to Muscovite officials and publicly executed.

Emelian Pugačëv was also a Don Cossack. In 1773, during the reign of Catherine II, he led an uprising of the Ural Cossacks which soon spread into a mass rebellion. Serfs, workers in the Ural mines and factories, Old Believers (a group opposed to the religious reforms of the Patriarch Nikon in the seventeenth century), and Tatars joined Pugačëv. He proclaimed himself Emperor Peter III, saying that he had escaped the plot of his wife Catherine. Peter was killed in a palace revolution instigated by Catherine in 1762. Pugačëv had established a kind of imperial court that was an imitation of the real one. In 1774 his troops were defeated and he was eventually handed over by his own men to the government and executed. Longworth (pp. 152, 206) discusses what both Razin and Pugačëv meant to the people. Razin was the last of the great Cossack pirates and the first great protestor against tsarist domination. He became a legend, and his name came to symbolize resistance of the government that stifled free spirit. "They did not wait for the Messiah, they waited for Stenka to return." Pugačëv exploited the messianic hopes of the people. He was presented as a king-savior and emphasized his origin from the Russian soil, playing on the people's opposition to the westernization introduced by Peter I at the beginning of the eighteenth century, and the series of emperors and empresses of foreign origin, such as Catherine, with their foreign advisers and foreign life style. Longworth describes him as a very colorful character: "Pugachev lived half in reality, half in a dream world. He would use high-sounding phrases one moment and coarse provincial epithets the next. . . . He would ride before his flock dressed like an emperor wearing the red sash of the Order of St. Anne under a handsome red coat" (p. 207).

Carl Stief, *Studies in the Russian Historical Song* (Copenhagen, 1953), p. 7, suggests that the particular mode of life and interests of the Cossack community fostered the historical song in which Cossack warriors and their achievements were celebrated, instead of singing the *byliny* celebrating the court life of Kiev. In his discussion of the songs about Ermak, Stief shows that the songs vary from short ones relating how Ermak was elected ataman, to a long poem with a detailed description of his conquest of Siberia.

16.   *Večerinka*—an evening party; *posidelka*—a winter evening party of young people in the village. They usually began in late autumn, when work in the fields was over. In *The Village of Viriatino,* one of the women describes these parties: "in the last two weeks of December, after the end of field work, ten to twelve girls from the neighborhood would get together in the evenings to spin and knit together . . . As they did their work, they chatted and listened to fairy tales told by elderly women. . . . Sometimes they would put the work aside briefly to dance and sing. Toward the end of the evening boys who had not left the village in search of seasonal work . . . would drop by. Usually the young men were not invited into the house but from time to time girls came outside to see them" (p. 140).

17.   N. P. Kolpakova (Russian Folk Songs of Everyday Life), pp. 54–84, discusses game songs at length. She points out that not every game song is a *xorovod,* and vice-versa. In a game the participants act out an episode of a plot, whereas in *xorovods* they usually dance in a circle, a chain, the figure 8, and so on, without acting out anything. Many games are based on rituals and work, and imitate activities such as sowing, reaping, and baking bread. The basic characteristic of game songs is action that is directly expressed, rather than a revelation of psychological states. They provide an uninterrupted development of action, with an uninterrupted series of movements. For example, agricultural game songs imitate sowing, plowing, and reaping; animal songs portray a duck swimming on the water, building her nest, leading her children. Usually love songs and family songs are based on double or triple repetition of the plot motif: a girl weaves a rug (prepares a bed, weaves a garland) carelessly for an old man and carefully for a young man; a young man sits down at a feast first opposite a young widow, then opposite a young girl. This kind of repetition emphasizes the contrast between the separate parts of the game. Kolpakova (p. 69) classifies the basic forms of the games: (I) a circle where everyone stands in place and performs the content of

the song with various movements; (2) pairs or rows, interweaving in the
process of performing imitative games like weaving, portraying the movement of a weaving shuttle, etc.; (3) two lines spread out, when two parties
of players in turn come together and move back from each other; a circle,
when everyone stands in place or moves in one direction or another,
while a work scene, love scene, or family scene is acted out in the middle.

18.   In the Orthodox church, icons, which are paintings on wooden
panels, take the place of statues as symbolic representations of holy
figures.

19.   Balašov and Krasovskaja describe the rituals that once took place
on the Tersk shore of the White Sea. In the matchmaking ritual the bride
was absent, and two matchmakers came to her parents' house. In the
majority of cases they were the godfather of the fiancé and the fiancé's
brother-in-law. The matchmakers improvised a conversation and allegorically praised the fiancé. They made the proposal in the evening and
gave the parents a night to decide. In the morning they would get their
answer (p. 26).
   For a good discussion of what customs have been lost in the marriage
ritual in modern Soviet society, and which have been added, see L. A.
Pushkareva and M. N. Shmeleva, "The Contemporary Russian Peasant
Wedding," *Introduction to Soviet Ethnography*, I, pp. 343–361.

20.   Balašov and Krasovskaja describe the version of *rukobit'e* that
took place in the Tersk area. Two matchmakers from the fiancé came
to the bride's house. The father and the first matchmaker, each wearing
a mitten on their right hand, took each other by the hand, and the second
matchmaker would beat them on their hands, after which everyone sat
down at the table. They lit the icon lamp under the icon while the bride
wailed on her bed in another room, and the rest ate a meal together.
The matchmakers then left, and in the evening the fiancé came with
the wedding ring (p. 28).

21.   The typical life of a married woman in the peasant village is
described in *The Village of Viriatino*. Women were responsible for all
the housework, the preparation of food, cleaning, washing, the care of
children, tending the cattle, and drawing water. During the autumn and
winter they spent all their free time spinning and weaving for their
family. They stacked hay, and at harvest they bound the sheaves and
helped with chain threshing. The daughter-in-law was in a particularly
difficult position. Her complete dependency on the family is illustrated
by a proverb that was well known in Viriatino: "Work—whenever it is
forced upon you; eat—whenever it is given to you" (p. 102).

22.   Ralston describes a variation of the *devičnik* described by Tereščenko in *Byt russakago naroda* [Manners and Customs of the Russian

People] II (St. Peterburg, 1848), pp. 126–130. When it grew dark, candles were lighted, and bread and salt and a *karavai*, a special cake, were placed on the table. The girls led the bride to a raised seat and sat around her. One of the girls wrapped the bride's head in a wedding veil and led songs in which they describe her departure from among them. They then took off the veil and began combing her hair. Unmarried Russian girls wore their hair in one long, single braid, a *kosá*. Its unplaiting was a sign of the change occurring, since married women wore their hair in two braids wound around their head and concealed under a kerchief. The girls rebraided her hair, and then sat at the table and sang a *karavai* song. The *krásota* ceremony would then take place and then the girls would leave (pp. 271–276).

23.   Y. Sokolov (p. 213) notes that sometimes the laments were performed by professionals, usually poor women, widows, or orphans. They composed the lament to reflect the experiences of the particular bride in whose name they were singing. These laments were a form of improvisation with a conventional poetics. Sokolov also mentions that in many areas the girls learned the wedding laments when they were still small, and after their betrothal they went to the "weepers" for instruction.

24.   The *družka* [best man], as Sokolov points out (p. 217), was a very important part of the ceremony. He was often the main director of the ceremonies, and took on the role of the medieval buffoons who were invited to weddings for entertainment. The best man was also supposed to protect the bride and groom from "spells" and from the "evil spirit." In Northern Russia he performed magical ceremonies, such as walking around the wedding train with a whip or a bell, and in his jests he included a number of magic incantations.

25.   Balašov and Krasovskaja describe a ceremony called *poniman'e* that took place in the Tersk area. This ceremony occurred before the bride and groom left for church. The bridegroom and his relatives arrived in an ordered procession, led by the best man. All the relatives sat down at the table, and the groom sat under the icon of the groom, which he had hung next to the bride's. The bride was in the next room putting on her bridal attire. As soon as the guests were seated, a choir, standing on benches, sang and then called for the bride. Her father led her out, and she and the groom drank wine. She said farewell to her relatives, and the bride and groom left for church.

In this region the people had the belief that the bride and groom were particularly vulnerable to sorcery just before the wedding, during the *poniman'e*. Therefore the couple always sat with a blank wall behind them, since it was believed that a sorcerer could "do harm" from behind, through a window. One woman who was "harmed" at her wedding lost seventeen kilograms during her first year of marriage—she could not sleep and had no appetite. In order to defend the couple from sorcery, an *otpusk*, a special incantation, was said over them while they stood under the icons (pp. 62–66).

Mary Matossian ("The Peasant Way of Life," in *The Peasant in Nineteenth-Century Russia*, ed. Wayne Vucinich [Stanford, 1968], p. 28) describes what took place on the day after the wedding: "The following morning Vladimir and Marfa are awakened by the best man and *svakha* [matchmaker], who collect Marfa's shift, now spotted with blood. Then they parade around this 'proof' of her premarital virginity, beating earthen pots. Vladimir and Marfa get up and take a ritual steam bath together. Having gathered at the Petrovs [parents of groom], the guests now go back to the Ivanovs [bride's parents] for the *chuloba* ritual. The first dish served is an omelette, which Vladimir tastes. Then he puts money in a glass of wine and gives it to Marfa Ivanov to make it understood that he regards Marfa as 'honorable.'"

The capture of the bride by the groom, as described by Propp, is a widespread phenomenon in many countries. An interesting discussion of it in Yugoslavia is Vesna Konstantinović's "The Abduction of a Bride as an Ethnosociological Phenomenon and Tradition Transformation among the Peoples of Yugoslavia in the 20th Century," *IXth International Congress of Anthropological and Ethnological Sciences* (1973), where she traces how what was once a custom based on sociological necessity later becomes mere entertainment. "Connubial capture" is also discussed by Ernest Crawley in *The Mystic Rose* (New York, 1960), pp. 76–100.

In his description of Igor Stravinsky's *Les Noces*, based on the songs of the Russian wedding ritual (Nonesuch recording) Eric Salzman notes that in this work there are no characters, but the solo singer and chorus take now one role, now another. "Everything is typical and convention-alized; we hear bits of ritual, the voice of the bride and bridegroom, scraps and bits of overheard conversation, invocations to Mary and the saints, descriptions of the wedding customs as they are acted out, stock phrases and clichés, peasant proverbs and allusions, superstitions and fragments of folk tales, bawdy comments by the guests, and the ritualized weeping of the bride." He also comments on the part folk melodies played in this piece: "The incessantly repeated figures, the focusing and re-focusing of static, triadic harmony, combined with the endless bits of chant and folk modal melos, all articulated by the changing rhythms, meters and accents, create a kind of ritualistic vision made of great, overlapping cycles, utterly objective and detached yet encompassing and enormous in scope." This piece is one instance of the influence of Rus-sian folk music on Stravinsky's work.

26.   Kolpakova (pp. 139–141) desribes the characteristic devices used in satiric songs. Their object was to create a grotesque figure, a caricature,

emphasizing all negative attributes. The basic device of the satiric song is irony: a husband brings home to his wife a "fine" present—a silken whip; a wife sews her husband a shirt "out of the finest cloth—out of nettles." Satiric hyperbole is also used: although supposedly ill, a wife beats her husband and then eats a bull, an ox, seven calves, and eight suckling pigs. Metaphoric epithets are also used to emphasize the grotesque. Examples are "fleecer, crooked-fingered, berrylike, sugary, baggy, samovar-like, creepy." They are also similes: a mother-in-law on the stove is like a bitch on a chain. Abusive words are also used for satiric effect: husband-devil, husband-fool, as well as endearing words used ironically— sweet little mother-in-law, auntie, dear, sweet husband.

27.   I. Repin (1844–1930) was a representative of the Realist movement in Russian art practiced by the group known as the Wanderers, who painted in the 1870's and 1880's. They reacted against the Petersburg Academy's demands to paint only historical and mythological themes and turned instead to painting the everyday reality of the middle class and lower class in contemporary Russia, and they admired Courbet and Millet in France, who were painting similar subjects in France.

Jerome Blum (*Lord and Peasant in Russia* [Princeton, 1961], p. 283) points out that the river system was expanded in the eighteenth and nineteenth centuries by state-built canals connecting major streams. Hundreds of thousands of workers were employed in shipping, and most of them served as human draught animals to pull the barges and boats upstream against the current. In 1815 an estimated 400,000 of these boatmen worked on the Volga. "The hardships and brutality of their occupation were so great that of these 400,000 an average of 7000 were said to have perished on the job each year, and thousands more returned to their villages ruined in health."

28.   I. N. Rozanov ("From Book to Folklore," in *The Study of Russian Folklore*, ed. Felix Oinas and Stephen Soudakoff [Bloomington, Indiana, 1971], pp. 101–116) discusses the relationship between original literary versions of poems which later became folk songs, and adaptations of folk songs by individual authors. Whereas in the Bogdanov version the cudgel was the symbol of Russian stagnation, in Ol'xin's version it becomes the weapon of the aroused masses.

29.   N. Aristova, in *Ob istoričeskom značenii russkix razbojničix pesen* [On the Historical Significance of Robber Songs] (Voronež, 1875), discusses the conditions under which the robbers had to live. Their life underwent constant change. One day they would be dressed in satin and velvet, the next in rags; one week they would be sleeping on a feather bed, then for a whole month on dirty bast matting. They were forced to live in caves and ravines, and in winter they sought refuge in the

villages but were often driven out. However, as Aristova points out (pp. 157–160), most of the songs emphasize the positive side of the robber's life, describing fine meals on silken tablecloths, amusing games, and clothes of velvet, with sable caps and boots of Moroccan leather. She also describes how difficult it was for a robber, used to a very free life, to exist in prison, and many of the robber songs about prison portray the sharp contrast between their former life and the confining life in a prison cell.

30. Kirša Danilov's collection of *byliny* was first published in 1804 and had undergone three reprintings by 1818. A recent edition is *Drevnie rossijskie stixotvorenija*, ed. A. P. Evgen'eva and B. N. Putilov (Moscow-Leningrad, 1958).

31. *Dubrovskij* (1832–1833), a novel, was never completed. Dubrovskij is the son of a landowner whose lands had been illegally seized by one of the neighboring gentry. The son turns robber, but in the tradition of the "noble robber" he robs the rich and gives to the poor. In the story one of the characters describes him: "I have always heard that Dubrovsky doesn't simply attack anybody, but only those who are known to be rich, and that even then he only takes his share, so as not to leave them destitute. And he's never been accused of murder" (*Dubrovsky: The Complete Prose Tales of Alexandr Sergeyevitch Pushkin*, trans. G. R. Aitken [New York, 1966], p. 229). The story includes a Romeo-Juliet theme. Dubrovsky falls in love with the daughter of the landowner who ruined his father, making it difficult for Dubrovsky to achieve his revenge.

32. *Kaptanskaja dočka* [The Captain's Daughter] (1833–1835), a historical novel, is written in the tradition of the historical novel of Sir Walter Scott. Historical events, in this case the Pugačëv Rebellion, are described in terms of how they affect the personal life of a young nobleman. Pugačëv is portrayed as capable of great cruelty and great magnanimity. His attitude toward the rebellion is: "Then you don't believe . . . that I am Tsar Pyotr Fyodorovitch? All right. But is not success for the bold? . . . One master's as good as another" (*The Captain's Daughter* in *The Complete Prose Tales of Alexandr Sergeyevitch Pushkin*, p. 409). The young hero sees Pugačëv as a tramp and, replete with honor, replies to Pugačëv's offer to join his band: "I am a nobleman by birth; I have sworn allegiance to my Sovereign Lady, the Empress: I cannot serve you" (p. 409). In 1834, Pushkin published a two-volume nonfiction work, *Istorija Pugačëva* [The History of Pugačëv], where Pugačëv is depicted with little of the sympathy shown in the fictional version of the leader of the rebellion.

33. M. K. Azadovskij in "Fol'kloristika XVIII v" [The Study of Folklore in the eighteenth century], *Russkoe narodnoe poètičeskoe tvorčestvo*

[Russian Folk Poetry] (Moscow, 1956), p. 52, says that M. D. Čulkov's collection of folk songs (1770–1774) contained both actual folk songs as well as literary imitations, but that he made a distinction between the two. He did not collect the songs himself, but relied on various manuscripts of collectors of songs. Many of the songs found in his collection, particularly in the fourth part, later disappeared, and in this sense the collection has important historical significance. As a literary figure, Čulkov is primarily remembered for his short story "Prigožaja povarixa, ili poxoždenie razvratnoj ženščiny" [The Comely Cook, or the Adventures of a Debauched Woman] (1770), written in the vein of *Moll Flanders*.

34. The songs about Stepan Razin and Pugačëv also belong to the genre of historical songs. V. K. Sokolova, in "Istoričeskie pesni" [Historical Songs], *Russkoe narodnoe poètičeskoe tvorčestvo*, [Russian Folk Poetry], ed. P. T. Bogatyreva, 2d ed. (Moscow, 1956), makes a distinction between the historical song and the epic. The historical songs are a later form of historical folk poetry and began to be widely developed in the sixteenth century. Instead of knights with superhuman strength, the heroes of historical songs are actual historical figures, such as Ivan IV, Peter I, Razin, and so on. The historical song does not have the breadth of the epic and does not describe every step of an event in detail. It concentrates on one central episode, and description is concise and precise. Although at first historical songs had many similarities to epic poetry, as they developed they took on many features of lyric folk poetry. The songs having an epic quality focus on the events themselves, whereas those with lyric qualities concentrate on the influence these events have on the major figures. They use symbol and epithet for emotional effect. Often there is a monologue describing the thoughts of the hero about the events taking place, about his fate (pp. 367–404).

35. Igor Stravinsky (*An Autobiography* [New York, 1962], p. 71), shows the influence of the recruiting songs on his composition *L'Histoire d'un soldat*: "This cycle of Russian tales from Afanasev's collection was based on folk stories of a cruel period of enforced recruitment under Nicholas I, a period which also produced many songs known as *Rekroutskia*, which expatiate in verse on the tears and lamentations of women robbed of their sons or sweethearts. Although the character of their subject is specifically Russian, these songs depict situations and sentiments and unfold a moral so common to the human race as to make an international appeal. It was this essentially human aspect of the tragic story of the soldier destined to become the prey of the Devil that attracted Ramuz and myself."

36. A. N. Radiščev (1749–1802) is an important representative of the literary period of Sentimentalism in Russia, in which the author's

feelings are the main focus of the work. In *Putešestvie iz Peterburga v Moskvu* [The Journey from St. Petersburg to Moscow] (1790) Radiščev describes the pity and horror aroused in him by the gentry's cruel treatment of the serfs, including the unjust process of recruitment. After Catherine II read it, she exiled Radiščev to Siberia. Blum calls the book "The most famous and outspoken attack on serfdom in the eighteenth century" (p. 562).

37. Conscription began with Peter I and became a permanent part of Russian life. As Blum points out (p. 465), the draft was made on the settlement rather than on the individual, and the village commune or the owner selected the number of recruits demanded, thus providing for much corruption and injustice in the process of recruiting. For most of the eighteenth century the term of service was for life. In 1793 it was reduced to twenty-five years, in 1834 to twenty years, and in 1855 to twelve years active service. To avoid the draft, serfs sometimes deliberately maimed themselves or were crippled as infants by their parents.

38. The Swedish king referred to is Charles XII, who in 1700 began his attack on Russia, and was successful at the Battle of Narva. This victory impelled Peter I to strengthen his forces, and in 1708, when Charles began to move south and enter the Ukraine, he and Peter fought the famous Battle of Poltava, in which the Swedish army was destroyed on July 8, 1709. By this victory Russia replaced Sweden as the major power in the North and became an important European power.

39. The Igor tale is a twelfth-century epic whose theme is the need for national unity among the princes against foreign attack. One of its most famous passages concerns the battle against the Polovtsians, the results of which are described in terms of sowing and reaping: "the black earth beneath the hooves was sown with bones and watered with blood: a harvest of sorrow came up over the land of Russia." From "The Lay of Igor's Campaign," *The Heritage of Russian Verse*, ed. Dimitri Obolensky (Bloomington: Indiana University Press, 1976), pp. 7–8.

40. Even after emancipation no peasant could lawfully leave his village without obtaining a passport, issued only with the permission of the village authorities, or the household elder, if the applicant was a junior member of the household. See Michael Florinsky, *Russia: A History and Interpretation* (New York, 1953), p. 895.

41. Pushkin wrote "Uznik" [The prisoner] in 1822.

> I sit behind bars in a damp prison.
> Reared in captivity, a young eagle,
> My melancholy comrade, flaps its wings,
> And pecks at its bloody prey under my window.

It pecks, then stops, and looks into my window.
As if thinking what I am thinking.
He beckons me with his look and cry
And he wants to say: "Let's fly away!
We are free birds; it's time, brother, it's time!
To where the mountain is turning white behind the clouds,
To where the boundless sea is turning blue,
To where only the wind roams . . . and I! . . .

42.   M. Ju. Lermontov's poem "Želan'e" [The Wish] was written in 1832:

>Unlock this dungeon for me,
>Grant me radiant days,
>A black-eyed maid,
>A black-maned horse.
>Let me gallop just once
>Along the blue field on that horse;
>Let me look just once at life and freedom,
>And on my strange fate
>So close to me.
>
>Give me a little wooden boat
>With rotten seats,
>A sail gray and tattered,
>Acquainted with storms.
>I'll set out then for the sea,
>Untroubled and alone,
>I'll wander on the vast sea
>And in a raging quarrel I'll amuse myself
>With the wild whim of the deep.
>
>Give me a tall palace
>Surrounded by a garden green,
>So that in its broad shadow
>An amber vineyard shall grow;
>So that a fountain never hushing
>Shall murmur in the marble hall
>And washing me with cold dust,
>Shall lull me and waken me
>While I dream of paradise.

43.   N. P. Ogarëv (1813–1877) was a friend and supporter of Alexander Herzen, whose socialist ideas had a great influence on Russian intellectuals in the 1840's and 1850's. Ogarëv was coeditor of *The Bell*, a weekly paper published in London and brought into Russia surreptitiously. His poetry is melancholy and sentimental.

44. Russian is a highly inflected language with an abundance of morphological endings. Rhymes that employ these endings become predictable and monotonous if used too frequently within one poem. Examples of this usage can be seen in a poem by Mixail Lomonosov written in the eighteenth century, whose title, translated, reads "An evening meditation on the divine Majesty on the Occasion of the Great Northern Lights":

> Usta premudryx nam glasjat:
> Tam raznyx množestvo svetov,
> Nesčetny solnca tam gorjat,
> Narody tam i krug vekov:
> Dnja obščej slavy Božestva
> Tam ravna sila estestva.   [II. 13–18]

The first and third lines end in verbal rhymes, [-at] being the third person plural present tense ending; the second and fourth lines have the noun ending [-ov], which is genitive masculine plural. In Propp's example, the rhymes are based on the verbal ending [-la], feminine singular past tense; his second example is based on the adjectival ending [-aja], nominative feminine singular.

45. Sokolov (p. 525) shows that this type of progression is usually formulaic. For example, in the sequence "one's own family" the sequence is: father, mother, young brothers and sisters. In the formula "another family," which appears in girls' songs describing their husband's home, the sequence is: father-in-law, mother-in-law, brothers-in-law, sisters-in-law.

46. Kolpakova (1962, p. 143) distinguishes between the different forms of exposition in narrative lyrics and ballads. Lyric narratives do not have a clear-cut plot, a strong dramatic conflict, a great sense of movement, or large, tragic themes. They are more peaceful, more melancholy, and often break off without finishing. They usually contain one episode of a plot, and the plot itself is less developed and simpler than in ballads. They concentrate on the individual subjective responses of the hero or heroine to the events, rather than on the events themselves.

47. Kolpakova (1962) has done a detailed typology of the symbols in Russian folk lyrics. For example, she classifies the various symbols for unhappiness (p. 231):

Unhappy love	Fog, rain, wind, dew. A tree rustles, twists, bends. Berries, flowers, grass are trampled, fruit falls from the trees. Overgrown paths, bridges smashed. The ominous cry of birds.

Parting with one's beloved	The sun does not rise, the moon is low. Fog, rain, snowstorm, ice, wind. Flooding river, turbid water, mud, dew. A tree rustles, bows down, dries up, is broken, falls. The birds are silent, fish tremble in nets.
Orphanhood	Moan of the sea, flooding rivers. Dried-up or broken tree. A straying bird, a lost feather. A stone.
Death	Sun setting, flame going out. Wind, rain, cloud, thunder, frost, snow, fog, dew, dust. Waves on the sea, the noise of a river, flooding water, mud. A damp, dark forest. A dried-up tree, sterile, without leaves. Grass withers, sways, freezes, is beaten by rain. Flowers are plucked; they wither. Sand, stone. A house is destoyed, a fence is broken.

She also does a typology of symbols connected with happiness, examples being (p. 217):

Youth, beauty, health	Shining sun, stars, dawn. Young tree, flower, ripe berry. Pretty bird.
Happy love	Burning flame. Picking plants, birds plucking berries. A bridge across the water. Breaking through walls, nets, gates.

Trees, flowers, grass, and other images take on happy or sad symbolic significance depending on their function within the context of each song. Various related feelings (death, unhappy love) often use the same symbols. For an interesting discussion of how the same symbols take on different meanings in different folk genres, see V. K. Sokolova, "Some Traditional Symbols in Slavonic Folk-Poetry," *IXth International Congress of Anthropological and Ethnological Sciences* (1973). For example, "the road" and "the unknown land" are mentioned in funerary as well as nuptial poetry.

48.   Palekh was one of the main centers for icon painting in Russia. It is now famous for the lacquer boxes produced by local artists.

49.   A. P. Evgen'eva provides an interesting analysis of the application of the epithet in oral poetry in *Očerki po jazyku russkoj ustnoj poèzii* [A Study of the Language of Russian Oral Poetry] (Moscow-Leningrad, 1963), pp. 298–338.
   For a detailed discussion of the fixed epithet in folk poetry, see P. D. Uxov, "Postojannye èpitety v bylinax kak sredstvo tipizacii i sozdanija obraza" [The Fixed Epithet in the Byliny as a Means of Typification and

the Creation of an Image], in *Osnovnye problemy èposa vostočnyx slavjan* [Basic Problems of the Epic of the Eastern Slavs] (Moscow, 1958), pp. 158–171. He notes that certain typical attributes of a phenomenon may change in the course of time; so, for example, the fixed epithet for sable may be black, Jakut, or Siberian. Fixed epithets also change according to the area which produces the folk poetry: in the Don Cossack epic tradition, the conventional "wide" steppe becomes the "wild" steppe, and the "wide" gate becomes the "lattice" gate. These epithets also change according to genre, so that the "heroic horse" of the *bylina* becomes a "black horse" in the lyric song. Uxov also points out that the fixed epithet in folk poetry is a means of typifying images, whereas an individualizing epithet is used in certain contexts to individualize the image. Thus the epithet "deep" modifying the word "river" does not actually mean a deep river in contrast to a shallow river, but it means a river in general; "green" wine means wine in general. When an individualized image is needed, a nonconventional epithet is substituted for the fixed epithet. The typical phrase for a young girl in folk poetry is *devica krasnaja* [pretty maid], which indicates she is a young girl, not a matron, and that she is a peasant. In one *bylina*, however, a girl of unusual beauty and intelligence is described as *poučënaja devica* [a learned maid], emphasizing her unusual qualities, rather than her typical ones.

50. *Lubok*—a broadside print, often used for popular social satire.

51. A. K. Tolstoj (1817–1875) is noted for his humorous verse and ballads. His most famous work is his satire *Kuzma Prutkov.*

52. Dmitrij Sadovnikov (1843–1883) wrote poetry about the Volga region. His most famous ballad is "Stenka Razin and the Persian Princess."

53. Nikolaj Nekrasov (1821–1878) was the almost important representative of socially conscious poetry in the second half of the nineteenth century. He wrote several narrative poems on peasant life, imitations of folk songs, and satires.

54. Reginald Zelnik in "The Peasant and the Factory," in *The Peasant in Nineteenth-Century Russia*, (Stanford, 1968), ed. W. S. Vucinich, pp. 158–190, says that the majority of workers in the factories at the beginning of the nineteenth century were manorial serfs, who took these jobs, with the permission of their lords, to use their wages to pay off their annual *obrok*. Their peasant status as opposed to worker status was reinforced by the fact that their sojourn in the city was temporary. They did not possess the legal right to own immovable property in the city, and most had no family life in the city (p. 181). After emancipation the

workers continued to have ties with the countryside. Labor legislation was introduced in Russia only in the mid-1880's, and even then the workers did not have the right to organize independently.

55.   The Altai Mountains are in eastern Siberia, along the Mongolian border.

56.   By 1762 there were over a hundred iron and copper plants in the Urals. Since the wages the owners were willing to pay were too low and the work too disagreeable for the local inhabitants to voluntarily take jobs, in 1734 the government issued a decree that any one starting an iron mill could get 100 to 150 families of state peasants assigned to his plant for each blast furnace he operated. If runaway serfs were hired, they became attached to the factories for the rest of their lives. Blum (p. 311) describes the conditions under which they had to work. The Ural plants had a workday of eleven hours in winter and thirteen hours in summer, and most full-time workers put in around 200 to 260 days a year. Women and children were widely employed. The enterprises that belonged to the state were run with military discipline, and little thought was given to the health and welfare of the workers. Conditions in privately owned plants were even worse. As Blum points out, one of the worst demands made on peasants assigned to plants in the Urals was the journey of many miles they had to make to perform their work obligation. "The thin settlement of the region compelled the manufacturers to draw the large contingents they needed for short-term employment from distant places. . . . In at least one case the peasants lived nearly 800 versts away [1 verst = 3500 feet]" (p. 313). Peasants without horses often spent 96 days a year on these journeys.

57.   The Demidovs were the most important industrialists of the Urals. Their reputation was so bad that in the eighteenth century the news that the Demidovs were going to take over a plant was enough to spark riots among the workers. Some of their employees in the nineteenth century tried to present petitions to the tsar and were either shot or thrown alive into a blast furnace (Blum, p. 313).

58.   P. V. Kireevskij was part of the Slavophile movement which flourished in the 1840's and 1850's in Russia. Its ideology centered around the belief in the superior nature and historical mission of Orthodoxy and Russia. They opposed the Western influence Peter I had introduced into Russia at the beginning of the eighteenth century, looking on it as an artificial imposition on the natural development of Russia, whose superiority lay in spirituality. Kireevskij published an important collection of folk songs from 1860 to 1874.

59.   The *kamarinskaja* is a lively Russian folk dance.

60.   Savva Morozov is an example of the patronage of the arts in Russia by the middle class. Morozov was an important factor in the founding of Stanislavsky's *Moscow Art Theater.*

61.   *Maëvka,* in prerevolutionary Russia, was a revolutionary meeting of workers on May 1.

62.   The Russo-Japanese War (1904–1905) was a disaster for Russia. There were physical difficulties, such as getting the Russian troops to the distant battlefield, but there were also more profound problems of morale: G. Vernadsky writes in his *History of Russia,* rev. ed. (New Haven, 1961), p. 239: "The Russian army went into battle without enthusiasm. The deep dissatisfaction of the Russian people with the government could not fail to be reflected in the army. The war was unpopular in Russia from the very beginning. . . . It did not seem to them to affect the vital interests of the country, while every Japanese soldier understood that vital interests of Japan were concerned."

63.   "Bloody Sunday" was a culmination of dissatisfaction exhibited by the Russian people in 1905. The workers went on strikes and the peasants rioted and soldiers revolted against their officers. A priest, Father Gapon, decided to lead the workers to the Winter Palace in St. Petersburg and appeal to the tsar for reforms. Although the crowd was unarmed, the soldiers fired on them and a large number of people were killed or wounded. This event came to symbolize the government's attitude toward the people.

PEASANT SONGS

Ritual Songs of the Agricultural Calendar

KOLJADKA SONGS

I

If you don't give us a tart—
We'll take your cow by the horns,
If you don't give us a sausage—
We'll grab your pig by his head,
If you don't give us a pancake—
We'll give the host a kick.

Ljadov, no. 3.

2

"Oh, *ovsen'*, oh *koljada*!
Is the master at home?"
"He's not at home,
He's gone to the field
To sow some wheat."
"May the wheat be sown,
Ears of grain,
Ears of grain,
Grains, little grains!"

Nekrasov, p. 6.

3

Koljada has come
On Christmas Eve.
Give us a cow,
A head full of butter!*
And may God give to the man
In this house
To him thick rye,
Plentiful rye:

*cow and a head full of butter—a ritual pastry in the form of farm animals (Tr.)

To him 100 liters of grain,
From one grain a loaf,
From half a grain a pie.
May the Lord allot you
Well-being and life
And riches,
And may the Lord create for you
All the very best!

Shein, no. 1032.

4

Koljada has come
Before Christmas
    My beautiful green vineyard!*
The gentle snow has fallen
The sparkling white snow;
And along this gentle snow
Geese-swans fly—
Koljada singers,
Young ones,
Young ones,
Pretty girls
Looking, searching
For Ivan's home,
And Ivan's home
Is not near, not far—
Not near, not far—
On seven columns;
Around this house
A silver paling stands;
Around this paling
Is silken grass;
On each pale
Is a little pearl.
Inside this paling
Three towers stand,
Three towers stand
With golden cupolas.
In the first tower—

* V. I. Čičerov suggests that the vineyard image in *koljada* songs is a symbol of fertility, growth, abundance, and also love and marriage (Propp, *Russkie agrarnye prazdniki* [Russian agricultural holidays], p. 38) (Tr.).

The moon shines,
In the second tower—
A lovely little sun,
In the third tower—
Little twinkling stars.
The moon shines—
Then the lord is at home,
A lovely little sun—
Then the hostess,
Little twinkling stars—
The little children.
But the lord himself*
Is not at home,
Not at home,
It can't be:
To Moscow he went
To make judgments in court,
To make judgments in court,
To arrange his affairs.
He did some judging, did some arranging,
Then home he came;
To his wife he brings
A coat of marten, a cap of marten,
And to his sons
A fine steed each,
And to his daughters
A gold wreath each,
To his servants
A pair of boots each.
Oh, our *koljada*
is not small, not large—
She doesn't climb through the door
But comes to our window:
Don't break, don't destroy it,
Give us a whole tart!
      My beautiful green vineyard!

Shein, no. 1030.

*Propp (*Russ. Agr. Hol.*, p. 43) suggests that the host is purposely described as noble and rich in this song, because the folk believed that by describing him in this way, he might become so. Thus he is portrayed here as going to court—legal procedure was once the privilege of princes and noblemen. His wealth is revealed by the kinds of gifts he brings home—furs, horses, gold wreaths.

PLATTER SONGS

5

The ring was rolling
Along the velvet,
The ring rolled up
To the ruby.

The one who takes it out—
For her will it come true,
For her will it come true—
She will not escape.

Shein, no. 1094. The song signifies a marriage.

6

A rooster was digging
On a *zaválinka**
The rooster dug up
A little pearl.
For whoever gets it,
All will be well!

Snegirev, vyp. 2, p. 84, no. 29.

7

A calyx is floating
From somewhere beyond the sea.
To wherever it floats,
There will it blossom.

Whoever takes it out
For her will it come true,
She will not escape.
          Glory!

Zemcovskij, no. 159.

*zaválinka—a small mound of earth along the outer walls of a peasant's house (Tr.).

8

A maple entwined with a birch*—
It did not untwine.
        Ladu, ladu!
Whoever takes it out
For her will it come true,
All will be well!

Zemcovskij, no. 174.

9

A little cat is sitting*
In a little wicker basket.
She is sewing a towel,
She will marry the tom.
For whom we are singing
All will be well!

Zemcovskij, no. 204.

10

A falcon flies**
From one street,
        Glory!
A little dove
From another.

They fly together
And kiss,

With their gray wings
They embrace.

To whom we are singing
All will be well,

Whoever takes it out
For her will it come true,

*These songs predict marriage (Tr.).
**This song predicts marriage. The refrain is repeated after every two lines (Tr.).

It will come true,
She won't escape.

Glory!

Zemcovskij, no. 195.

II

The sleigh stands*
Ready to go,
        Glory!
In it the cushions
Are all arranged.
        Glory!
It stands near the forest,
Wanting to go for a ride.
        Glory!
To whom we sing this song,
All will be well,
It will come true,
She will not escape.
        Glory!

Zemcovskij, no. 261.

12

I sat**
By a window,
I waited
For my beloved,
I couldn't
Wait anymore,
I fell asleep.
In the morning I awoke—
I suddenly realized—
I am a widow.

*This song predicts a journey (Tr.).
**This song predicts widowhood (Tr.).

To whom we sing
All will be well
All will come true
And she won't escape.

Zemcovskij, no. 280.

13

A dandy once took*
A very sharp ax,
          Lileju!
The dandy went out
Into the wide courtyard,
The dandy began
To hew some boards,
To nail the wood
Into an oaken coffin.
Whomever this song reaches
For her will it come true,
She will not escape.

Zemcovskij, no. 304.

14

With spades they are digging,**
With hatchets they are chopping,
          Iljeju, iljeju!
For whom we sing,
For her will it come true,
For her will it come true,
She will not escape,
          Iljeju, iljeju!

Zemcovskij, no. 317.

15

Death is walking down the street†
Carrying pancakes on a plate.

---

*This is performed at midnight on New Year's Eve. It predicts death (Tr.).
**This song predicts death (Tr.).
†This song also predicts death (Tr.).

Whoever takes the ring out—
  For her will it come true,
    Will come true,
    She will not escape.

Shein, no. 1136.

MASLENICA

16

We are waiting for Maslenica,
We are waiting, sweetheart, we are waiting,
Cheese and butter will we see before us,
Will we see, sweetheart, will we see.
On the mountain is a little green oak,
Green, sweetheart, green.
And the Veržin priest is young,
Young, sweetheart, young.
The priests' wives were drinking,
And they ruined the priests by drinking on a holiday,
On a holiday, sweetheart, on a holiday.
And the sextons' wives were drinking
And they ruined the sextons by drinking on a holiday,
On a holiday, sweetheart, on a holiday.
And the sacristans' wives were drinking
And they ruined the sacristans by drinking on a holiday,
On a holiday, sweetheart, on a holiday.

Rimsky-Korsakov, no. 46.

17

Our dear Maslenica,
Dear, lëli, dear!

Came for a while,
For a while, lëli, for a while.

We thought for seven weeks.
Seven weeks, lëli, seven weeks.

But Maslenica stayed only seven days,
Seven days, lëli, seven days.

And Maslenica deceived us,
Deceived us, lëli, deceived us.

To Lent she offered a seat,
Offered a seat, lëli, offered a seat.

Bitter horseradish she put out,
Put out, lëli, put out.

And that horseradish is more bitter then xren,*
More bitter than xren, lëli, more bitter than xren.

Zemcovskij, no. 380.

INVOCATIONS TO SPRING

18

Oh, little bee,
Ardent bee!
Fly out beyond the sea,
Get out the keys,
The golden keys.
Lock up winter,
Cold winter!
Unlock summer,
Warm summer,
Warm summer,
A summer fertile in grain!

Shein, no. 1181.

19

Oh, larks, dear larks!
Come fly to us,
Bring us
The warm summer,

* Xren—another type of horseradish (Tr.).

Take from us
The cold winter;
We are fed up
With cold winter,
Our hands and feet are frostbitten.

Aničkov, p. 93.

20

Little lark,*
Little lark!
For you winter,
For us summer!
For you a sleigh,
For us a wagon!

Zemcovskij, no. 410.

21

O little sun, fine weather
Come out, pretty one
From behind the mountain!
Come out, little sun,
It's springtime!
Oh, fine weather, have you seen
The beautiful spring?
Oh, pretty one, have you met
Her sister?
Oh, little sun, have you seen
The old hag,
The old gossip—
The witch-winter?
And so cruel, she ran away
From spring,
From beautiful spring she ran,
And collected cold frost in a bag,
And shook up the cold on the earth,
Then stumbled
and rolled down the hill.

Zemcovskij, no. 435.

*Sung on March 9th (Tr.).

GAME SONGS ABOUT SOWING

22

"Oj, millet we have sown, we have sown,*
Oj lid-lado, we have sown, we have sown!"

"And millet we will thresh, will thresh,
Oj lid-lado, we will thresh!"

"And with what will you thresh, will you thresh?
Oj lid-lado, will you thresh, will you thresh?

"And the horses we'll let out, let out,
Oj lid-lado, we'll let out, we'll let out!"

"And the horses we will catch, will catch,
Oj, lid-lado, we will catch, will catch!"

"And with what will you catch them, will you catch them?
Oj, lid-lado, will you catch them, will you catch them?"

"With a silken rein, a rein,
Oj lid-lado, with a rein, a rein!"

"And the horses we will ransom, will ransom,
Oj lid-lado, we will ransom, will ransom!"

"And with what will you ransom, will you ransom?
Oj lid-lado, will you ransom, will you ransom?"

"We will give 100 rubles, 1000 rubles,
Oj lid-lado, 100 rubles, 100 rubles!"

"We don't need a thousand, a thousand,
Oj lid-lado, a thousand, a thousand!"

---

*Ralston (p. 283) says that this song represents the custom of purchasing the bride. The singers from two choirs face each other and exchange questions and answers. After "What we want is a young maid" one of the girls in the second choir goes over to the first, the two sides singing respectively, "Our band has diminished" and "our band has increased." The game lasts until all the girls have gone over from one side to the other. Ralston suggests that "lado" may refer to a pagan deity of spring and love, Lado. However, M. F. Mur'janov in "Mif o Lade" [The Myth about Lado], *Russkij fol'klor* [Russian folklore], XII (Leningrad, 1971), 220–225, states that it is still impossible today to give the exact name of the ancient Slavic goddess of love (Tr.).

"Then what do you need, do you need?
Oj lid-lado, do you need, do you need?"

"We need a young maid, a young maid,
Oj lid-lado, a young maid, a young maid."

"Our band has diminished, diminished,
Oj lid-lado, diminished, diminished!"

"Our band has increased, increased,
Oj lid-lado, increased, increased!"

In our band we pour tears, pour tears,
Oj lid-lado, we pour tears, pour tears."

"In our band we drink beer, drink beer,
Oj lid-lado, we drink beer, drink beer!"

Novikova, p. 236, no. 176. Transcription 1935. Later in the song, threshing is understood as damage done to a field by animals, provoking the capture of the horse and the necessity of redeeming it. The ransom of a girl had a part in the ancestral way of life. (Propp).

23

Beneath the oak grove is flax, flax,
Beneath the green grove is flax, flax.
"Already have I sown, sown the flax,
And I kept repeating,
With my boots I beat it down,
On all sides I turned it:
Turn out well, turn out well, my flax,
Turn out well, my white flax,
Catch someone's fancy, my darling!"

    "Teach me, mama,
    How to weed the flax."
    "Well, this is how, daughter,
    This is how, daughter of mine,
    This is how, little dove,
    This is how, little dove."

"I weeded, weeded the flax,
I weeded, kept repeating,
Beat it down with my boots,
On all sides I turned it:
Turn out well, turn out well, my flax,

Turn out well, my white flax,
Catch someone's fancy, my darling!"

"Well, I have pulled, pulled up the flax,
Well, I kept repeating,
Beat it down with my boots,
On all sides I turned it:
Turn out well, turn out well, my flax,
Catch someone's fancy, my darling!"

"Well, I have spread the flax, I have spread the flax,
I have spread it, I kept repeating,
Beat it down with my boots,
On all sides I turned it:
Turn out well, turn out well, my flax,
Turn out well, my white flax,
Catch someone's fancy, my darling!"

"I dried out, dried out the flax,
I dried it out, I kept repeating,
Beat it down with my boots,
On all sides I turned it:
Turn out well, turn out well, my flax,
Turn out well, my white flax,
Catch someone's fancy, my darling!

"Well, I have trampled, have trampled the flax,
Well, I have trampled it, I kept repeating,
Beat it down with my boots,
On all sides I turned it:
Turn out well, turn out well, my flax,
Turn out well, my white flax,
Catch someone's fancy, my darling!

"I swingled, swingled the flax,*
I swingled, I kept repeating,
Beat it down with my boots,
On all sides I turned it:
Turn out well, turn out well, my flax,
Turn out well, my white flax,
Catch someone's fancy, my darling!

---

*Swingled—flax is beaten or swingled (scraped) with a wooden, swordlike tool called a swingle (Tr.).

I combed, combed the flax,
I combed, I kept repeating,
Beat it down with my boots,
On all sides I turned it:
Turn out well, turn out well, my flax,
Turn out well, my white flax,
Catch someone's fancy, my darling!

Well, I have spun, I have spun the flax,
Well, I have spun, I kept repeating,
I beat it down with my boots,
On all sides I turned it:
Turn out well, turn out well, my flax,
Turn out well, my white flax,
Catch someone's fancy, my darling!"

Shein, no. 388. Shein says, "The participants, predominantly girls, stand in a circle. In the middle one of them performs to the singing of the song; she begins to dance and express in pantomime all the procedures of processing the flax which the song relates." Every stanza is preceded by the six-line "Teach me, mother, how to weed the flax" (pull it, spread it, dry it, etc.) with the standard repetition, "Well, this is how, etc." It is given only once here (Propp).

ST. GEORGE'S SONGS*

We got up very early,
Washed our white faces,
Walked around the fields
Put up crosses,
Invoked Egor':
Brave Egor',
Macarius the saint!
Protect our flocks,
Every animal—
In the field and beyond the field
In the forest and beyond the forest
For you wolf, bear,
Old beast,
Fox and hare—
a stump and a log
At the edge of the forest!

*These three songs are selected from Zemcovskij, pp. 313–314, 316.

If they are given something:

> Thank you, auntie,
> For a good word
> For a nice gift!
> May God grant you
> 100 bulls—one year old
> 200 calves
> All one year old

If they are not given anything:

> You mean old lady,
> Stump and log,
> At the edge of the forest!
> Go to Tatarus [Hell]
> Return again,
> Pass through the damned mountains
> Don't find your way back!

We walked around the field
Invoking Egor',
Praising Markarius:
You, our brave Egory,
Macarius the saint!
Save our flocks
In the field and beyond the field
In the forest and beyond the forest,
Under the bright moon
Under the beautiful sun,
From the nasty wolf,
From the mean bear,
From the sly beast!

The willow came
From beyond the sea,
The willow brought
Health.
The willow whipped,
Beat to tears!
Once again to your health!
Up to the red egg!

SEMIK SONGS

24

Yo, yo, little birch,
Oh, oh, curly one!
Semik so honorable and Trinity—
It's only, only
Us, us girls
Who are having a holiday!

Shein, no. 1203. It is sung while selecting a birch for this holiday (Propp).

25

Oh birch so curly,
Curly and young,
Under you, little birch,
No poppy is blooming,*
Under you, little birch,
No fire is burning.
No poppy is blooming—
Pretty maids
Are dancing a *xorovod*,
About you, little birch,
They are singing songs.

Bogatyrev, p. 232. The folk curl and decorate the birch while singing this song (Propp).

26

Don't rejoice, oak trees,
Don't rejoice, green ones!
Not to you are the girls coming,
Not to you the pretty ones;
Not to you are they bringing pies,
Pastries, omelettes.
Yo, yo, Semik and Trinity!
Rejoice, birches,
Rejoice, green ones!
To you are the girls coming,

---

*No poppy is blooming—an example of the negative metaphor so often used in oral
poetry (Tr.).

To you are they bringing pies,
Pastries, omelettes.
Yo, yo, Semik and Trinity!

Tereščenko, VI, p. 164.

27

Well, dear *kuma,* we are becoming *kumas,**
    Aj ljuli, aj ljuli, we are becoming *kumas.*
We will become *kumas,* let us kiss,
    Aj ljuli, ljuli, let us kiss.
Come, *kuma,* let's eat *kisel',*
    Aj ljuli, let's eat *kisel'.***

Rimsky-Korsakov, no. 50.

28

I, a young girl, am going to the quiet meadow, the
    quiet meadow,
To the quiet meadow, to a little birch.
I, a young girl, will pluck a blue cornflower,
A little blue flower, a cornflower;
I, a young girl, will weave a wreath,
I, a young girl, will go to the river,
I will throw the wreath down the river,
I will think about my sweetheart:
My wreath is drowning—drowning,
My heart is aching—aching;
My wreath will drown,
My sweetheart will abandon me.

Vil'boa, no. 68 (Sobolevskij, V, no. 8).

29

In the garden—little garden,
Maidens are strolling,
    My snowball bush, my raspberry bush!
In the garden they picked flowers;
And wove wreaths.

Kuma—the song is an example of the songs sung during the *kuma* ceremony that takes place during Semik, when girls become *kumas,* or "adopted sisters," after kissing through wreaths (Tr.).

**kisel'*—a puréed fruit dessert (Tr.).

They tossed the wreaths
Into the Danube, into the rapid river;

Whoever's wreath floats,
That one will marry.
     My snowball bush, my raspberry bush!

Šišonko, p. 175 (Sobolevskij, II, no. 175).

KUPALA

30

Let's go, girls,
Let's go, girls,
Out to the grain,
Out to the grain.

In our grain,
In our grain,
Sits a witch,
Sits a witch.

"Get out, witch,
Get out, witch,
Get out of our grain,
Get out of our grain.

"Our grain,
Our grain
Has been consecrated,
Has been consecrated!

"Go away, witch,
Go away, witch,
To Sen'kovo,
To Sen'kovo,—
There the grain,
There the grain
Has not been consecrated,
Has not been consecrated."

Transcribed by S. V. P'jankovaja, 1969. The folk sing this song as they light the ear of corn—
part of the ritual of *Kupala* night. The song appears in Zemcovskij, no. 635.

31

Young maids, old ladies—
To the Kupala!
    Ladu-ladu
    To the Kupala!

Oh, whoever won't go
To the Kupala,
    Ladu-ladu,
    To the Kupala!

Oh, she'll become
A stump, a log,
    Ladu-ladu,
    A stump, a log!

And whoever goes
To the Kupala
    Ladu-ladu,
    To the Kupala!

She will become
A white birch tree!
    Ladu-ladu,
    A white birch tree!

Transcribed 1967 by a student expedition from Leningrad University; Zemcovskij, no. 637.

HARVEST

32

Oh, and glory to God,
That they have harvested the grain,
That they have harvested the grain
And put it in shocks,
On the threshing floor in stacks,
In the storeroom in cornbins,
And in the stove as tarts.

Shein, no. 1281.

33

Peter's wife
Early one morn
to her cornfields she went;
Daughters-swans,
Brides-quails
Out with her she led.
"Harvest, brides,
Harvest, daughters,
Daughters—swans,
Brides—quails!
Early in the morning,
Late in the evening—
To live well,
To live in harmony."

Shein, no. 1276.

Songs of
Peasant Slavery

34

In the forest, the forest thick
There sings, sings a little nightingale,
There cuckooes a bitter cuckoo,
And no one listens to her voice—
Only the little orphan girl listens,
The little orphan girl, the hay girl:
"My own mother, madame!
Ransom me out of slavery,
Out of slavery—out of the lord's house:
My frisky feet are worn out with standing,
My white arms are worn out with moving,
Rocking the lord's child."
"Well, my sweet child!
You're no golden treasure for us.
Bear it, don't speak of sorrow:
You'll bear it and you'll love it;
Wear dresses, don't wrinkle them:
If you wear out a dress, it is possible to make another,
And they say to bear sorrow is also possible."

Kireevskij, n.s., issue 2, pt. 2, no. 2676.

35

You curls, oh my curls,
Curls well-combed,
Oh, they lie on my shoulders
And want to uncurl.
Oh, a distant strange place
Curled, curled them.
Oh, our Obozer village
Our Obozer village
Cried and grieved,
For it wasn't allowed to take a long walk.
The evil boyar-lord
Ravaged our land.
And he, the evil one, chose

Our young fellows,
Our young fellows
For soldiers,
And us, beautiful girls,
For servants,
Young married women
For wet nurses,
And mothers and fathers
For work.
Our young men collected
On a steep hill,
Our young men refused
Their boyar-lord,
"You, our evil lord,
We are not your soldiers,
Our beautiful girls
Are not your servants,
Our young married women
Are not wet nurses
And our fathers and mothers
Are not workers."

Shein, *Serfdom*, p. 491. Transcribed 1862.

36

Once in the city of Ustjužin,
In the village of Denisova,
At the peasants Dolgogreevs'
Appeared a punitive expedition,
An expedition of the white tsar,
The white, Orthodox tsar.
Brave soldiers approached,
Brave garrison soldiers.
The quarters were decorated,
Soldiers were posted,
Not for a long time—for two months.
And a beautiful summer passed,
Not one girl appeared.
The young men hid
In the dark forests;
They abandoned their huts,
Left small children,
Young wives—to human shame.
Bear it, small children,
You stand firm, young wives,

Bear it, afterward we'll be able to love.
Gather in one place,
On the island of Kostyžnica,
And we will write a petition of one blood,
Of one blood and one tear.
We will choose a messenger,
By the name of Trifon Petrovič:
Go, brother of ours,
Don't regret your anguish-work,
Go to Peter's city,*
To Peter's city on the Neva River,
On the Neva River there stands the palace
Of the white Orthodox tsar;
You give, give the petition
To the white Orthodox tsar.

Shein, *Serfdom*, p. 692.

37

The snowball bush and the raspberry bush were drenched with
    water—
At that time mama gave birth to me.
Without collecting her thoughts, she gave me in marriage.
I had not been to visit mama for three years.
In the fourth year I decided to go.
I will change-transform myself into a bitter little bird,
Bitter will I fly to mama's garden,
Bitter will I sit on the sweet apple tree:
With bitter tears the whole garden will I drench,
With bitter laments my life, my heart will I dry up.
And mama will walk along the new passages,
The brides-swallows will she awaken:
"Brides, swallows, get up quickly!
Why is a bird singing in our garden?
Where is she, bitter bird, lamenting?"
My oldest brother will say: "Let's shoot it!"
My middle brother will say: "Let's catch it!"
But my youngest brother will say: "Why has she come to us?
Isn't she our bitter sister from a far-off land?
Come, bitter sister, up to our high tower.
Tell us about your sorrow, ask us about ours:

*Peter's city—St. Petersburg (Tr.).

How they are taking daddy and mama beyond the Volga,
Oldest brother they are turning into a soldier,
And middle brother's hair they'll crop for a lacky,
And youngest brother—turn into a shop assistant."

Shein, no. 852. Transcription from the 1860's.

38

"Oh, my lord, Sidor Karpovič,
How old are you?"
"Seventy, old lady, seventy,
Seventy, Paxomovna, seventy."
"Oh, my lord, Sidor Karpovič,
How many children do you have?"
"Seven, Paxomovna, seven!"
"Oh, my lord, Sidor Karpovič,
What will they eat?"
"Bread, old lady, bread,
Bread, Paxomovna, bread."
"Oh, my lord, Sidor Karpovič!
Where will they get bread?"
"Out in the world, old lady, out in the world,
Out in the world, Paxomovna, out in the world."
"Oh, my lord, Sidor Karpovič!
You go out in the world, and the dogs will eat you!"
"With a stick, old lady, with a stick,
With a stick, Paxomovna, with a stick."
"Oh, my lord, Sidor Karpovič!
It's winter out in the world, your feet will freeze."
"In bast sandals, old lady, in bast sandals,
In bast sandals, Paxomovna, in bast sandals."

Shein, no. 1010 (Sobolevskij, VII, no. 469).

Vocal Songs about Love

39

Along the meadow, along the little meadow water flows,
Along the little green meadow runs a golden stream,
And on stream after stream, a white swan is floating,
The white swan is a lovely, beautiful maiden;
And the gray drake is a fine young man.
When the maid sees the young man, she will be filled
      with joy,
A blush will spread over her white face.

Varencov, p. 57 (Sobolevskij, IV, no. 243).

40

Katjušen'ka was sitting
In a new chamber alone;
My Katen'ka was sewing
Delicate white sleeves;
Having sewn the sleeves,
To her father in the tower she went:
"Oh, father dear,
You think about me!"
"I'm thinking and keep thinking,
Go into a convent, Katja!"
"Oh, father dear,
For a convent I'm not fit—
The old Mother Superior's cassocak
Will I tear,
As for the young priest—
I'll set fire to his cheeks,
The young nuns—
I'll defile them all,
Indeed, I'll defile them all."
Out of St. Peter came a merchant
And wooed Katen'ka—
He praised and kept praising
His way of life:
"I, a young man, have
One and a half hundred ships!"
"I think and keep thinking—

I'll not marry this one!"
Out of Moscow came a general
And wooed Katen'ka.
He praised and kept praising
His way of life:
"I, a young man, have
One and a half hundred peasant souls!"
"I think and keep thinking—
I'll not marry this one!"
Out of a tavern came a musician

And wooed Katen'ka
He praised and kept praising
His way of life:
"I, a young man, have
Only a fiddle and whistle!"
"I think and keep thinking—
This one will I marry.
Whether I'll be full or not full—
I'll always be merry,
I'll walk out on the street—
I'll have honor and praise,
Honor will I have and praise,
A musician's wife!"

Shein, no. 597.

41

I said to my dear sweetheart,
Tearfully, complaining, I begged my dear sweetheart:
"Don't marry, my dear-tender sweetheart, don't marry,
As long as I live, now, a pretty maid, I will not marry."
My dear tender sweetheart wouldn't listen to me—he married,
Not a lovely, pretty maid,
But a bitter, ill-fated widow.
He inflamed, inflamed my soul,
Dropped, unleashed a spark of flame into my heart.
"Well, enough, my soul, of grieving and crying!
No matter how much you have cried, it is time to stop:
It is not for you to fill the blue sea with tears,
For you to sow the bare field with pining and anguish,
For you to comfort your dear sweetheart with words."
The pretty maid walks and strolls along the shore,
She steps from stone to stone, the young girl,
She clicks stone against stone.

Not in every gray stone is a fire, a flame,
Not in every fine young man is there real truth.

Kireevskij, n.s., issue 2, pt. 1, no. 1245.

42

It is not a falcon flying along the heavens,
It is not a falcon shedding gray feathers—
A young man is galloping down the road,
Bitter tears are pouring from his clear eyes.
He has said farewell to his native land,
From the low country,
Where Mother Volga flows in all her beauty.
He has said farewell to his pretty maid:
He has left her a precious ring with diamonds to remember
    him by;
In exchange he has taken from the pretty maid
A golden wedding ring;
And while they were exchanging, he spoke:
"Don't forget me, my dear,
Don't forget me, my darling!
The more often you look at my ring,
The more often will I kiss yours,
Pressing it toward my ardent heart,
Remembering you, my darling:
If ever I think about another love—
Your golden ring will come unsoldered,
If you go under the wreath with another*—
From my ring the stone will fall."

Shein, no. 759.

43

"Ah, why, little dove, are you sitting so unhappy
So unhappy are you sitting and so sad?"
"How can I, a little dove, be happy,
Be happy and joyful?

---

*Under the wreath—Timothy Ware, *The Orthodox Church* (Middlesex, England, 1964),
p. 304, says, "The second part of the marriage service culminates in the ceremony of
coronation: on the heads of the bridegroom and bride the priest places crowns, made among
the Greeks of leaves and flowers, but among the Russians of silver or gold. This, the
outward and visible sign of the sacrament, signifies the special grace which the couple
receive from the Holy Spirit, before they set out to found a new family or domestic Church.
The crowns are crowns of joy, but they are also crowns of martyrdom, since every true
marriage involves an immeasurable self-sacrifice on both sides" (Tr.).

Last evening a pretty dove was with me,
A pretty dove, who sat by me,
In the morning my dove lay slain,
Lay slain, shot!"

"Ah, why, young man, are you sitting so unhappy,
So unhappy are you sitting and so sad?"
"How can I, a young man, be happy,
Be happy and joyful?
Yesterday a pretty maiden was with me,
A pretty maiden, who sat by me,
She spoke lovely words and gave me her hand,
And gave me her hand in marriage,
And now the maid is being given away in marriage,
Given away in marriage, promised in marriage.

Gurilev, p. 58.

44

Oh, valley of mine, little valley,
        Oh, wide valley!
In that valley
        Grew a snowball bush,
On that snowball bush
        A cuckoo was crying.
"About what, my little cuckoo,
        About what are you cuckooing?
About what, my poor creature,
        About what are you grieving?
"And how can I, a little cuckoo,
        How can I not cuckoo?
And how can I, a poor creature,
        How can I not grieve?
One green garden there was,
        And it is drying up,
One dear friend had I,
        And he is leaving.
Alone, a young girl,
        Alone, he is abandoning me."

Shein, no. 764.

45

"Why, bitter cuckoo,
Why are you cuckooing?"
"How can I, a bitter cuckoo,
How can I stop cuckooing?
There was a green garden,
And it has withered!
In that garden was a little nightingale,
And it flew away!"
"Why, pretty girl,
Why are you crying and grieving?"
"How can I, a pretty girl,
Stop crying, stop grieving?
There was one, only one beloved,
And he has forsaken me!
To everyone, ah, yes, my beloved
To everyone he has said farewell
But of me, the young man, of me
Was he ashamed!
From half down the path, from the road
He turned back,
To me, a pretty girl,
To me he said goodby:
"Goodby, farewell, my beloved,
Goodby, God be with you!"
"If you find someone better, beloved,
You will forget me;
If you find someone worse, my beloved,
You will remember me!"

Kireevskij, n.s., issue 2, pt. 2, no. 2142.

Xorovod, Game, and Dance Songs about Love

RECRUITING FOR THE *XOROVOD*

46

By a garden-vineyard
Ran a road.
Along this road
A little girl walked,
Walked a little girl,
On her a scarlet fur coat,
Trimmed with beaver,
She had black brows.
She walks and walks,—
"Please come to the *xorovod!*"

Shein, no. 301.

47

Along the meadows spreads the grass.
What grass, what turf!
What bold young men!
What beautiful maids!
I love you, I will take you to the *xorovod,*
To the *xorovod* will I take a pretty maid,
A pretty maid for myself will I take.

Shein, no. 292.

XOROVOD, GAME, AND DANCE SONGS

48

Once they invited a young man,
They honored the brave fellow,
    My Dunaj, Dunaj,
    Son Ivanovič Dunaj!

To sit as a guest at a feast,
To watch the conversation.
They sat the young man down,
They sat the brave fellow down
Opposite a widow on a bench,
Opposite a bitter woman on a pine bench.
I will glance at the widow,
I will sigh heavily;
My downy cap will I take off,
Opposite the widow will I throw it.
"Ah, you, widow, well,
Bitter lady, pick it up!"
"I sir, am not your servant,—
I will not obey you!"
Then I will pick up the cap myself,
And put it on my head...
Once they invited a young man,
They honored the brave fellow...
They sat the young man down,
They sat the brave fellow down
Opposite a girl on a little chair,
Opposite a beauty on a leather-strapped chair,
I will glance at the girl,
I will sigh lightly;
My downy cap will I take off,
Opposite the girl will I place it.
"Ah, you, girl, well,
Pretty one, pick it up!"
"I am your servant, sir—
I will obey you:
I will pick up the downy cap,
Will comb your black curls,
Will comb your black curls,
Will put on the downy cap,
Will put on the downy cap,
Will kiss you and embrace you!"
      Dunaj mine, Dunaj,
      Son Ivanovič Dunaj!

Guljaev, p. 249 (Sobolevskij, IV, no. 122). The song is performed at parties in a peasant hut. "While singing this song, the players form a circle or sit down in place; one young man goes into the middle and, acting in accordance with the words of the song, takes off his hat or cap and puts it in front of a widow, and if one does not happen to be at the party, then in front of a man; the widow pushes the hat away; the young man, putting it on, takes it off again and puts it in front of a girl, who picks it up, smooths down the hair of the young man, puts the hat on him and then kisses him, and the game is finished or begun again" (Guljaev, p. 251). The refrain is repeated every two lines (Propp).

49

In the meadows, in the meadows,
In the meadows, the green meadows,
There grew, there grew,
There grew silken grass,
There bloomed, there bloomed
There bloomed azure flowers.
With that grass, with that grass,
With that grass will I feed my horse,
Will I feed, will I feed,
Will I feed him and stroke him.
I will take, will take,
Will take my horse to daddy.
"Daddy, daddy,
Oh, daddy of mine!
Receive, receive,
Receive my caressing words,
Look favorably on these friendly words:
Don't give, don't give,
Don't give me in marriage to an old man!
An old man, an old man,
To the death will I not love an old man,
With an old man, with an old man,
With an old man I will not take a stroll!"
In the meadows, in the meadows,
In the meadows, the green meadows,
There grew, there grew,
There grew silken grass.
There bloomed, there bloomed,
There bloomed azure flowers.
With that grass, with that grass,
With that grass will I feed my horse,
Will I feed, will I feed,
Will I feed him and stroke him.
I will take, will take,
Will take my horse to daddy.
"Daddy, daddy,
Oh, daddy of mine!
Receive, receive,
Receive my caressing words,
Look favorably on these friendly words:
Don't give, don't give,
Don't give me in marriage to a young boy!

A young boy, a young boy,
To the death will I not love a young boy,
With a young boy, with a young boy
With a young boy will I not take a stroll!"
In the meadows, in the meadows,
In the meadows, the green meadows,
There grew, there grew,
There grew silken grass.
There bloomed, there bloomed,
There bloomed azure flowers.
With that grass, with that grass,
With that grass will I feed my horse,
Will I feed, will I feed,
Will I feed him and stroke him.
I will take, will take,
Will take my horse to daddy.
"Daddy, daddy,
Oh, daddy of mine!
Receive, receive,
Receive my caressing words,
Look favorably on these friendly words:
Give me, give me,
Give me in marriage to one my own age!
One my own age, one my own age,
One my own age will I love with all my soul,
With one my own age, one my own age,
With one my own age will I take a stroll."

Prač, p. 180 (Sobolevskij, II, no. 299). In every stanza, every even line from the second to the fourteenth, and also every nineteenth, twenty-first, and twenty-third line is repeated. For extensive commentary by E. V. Gippius, see Balakirev, pp. 313–315, and Z. D. Eval'd in Gippius and Eval'd, *Pesni Pinež'ja* [Songs of Pinež'e], bk. 2, pp. 503–506 (Propp).

50

Brave tsar's son,
Why are you walking-strolling?
Brave tsar's son,
What do you see
Brave tsar's son?
"I am walking, walking and strolling,
I am walking and I see
My tsarevna
My queen.
And my tsarevna,
And my queen

Is strolling in Novgorod,
She wears a shining crown,
She wears a silk-embroidered sarafan."

"Go, tsar, to the city,
Take her by the hand,
Bow low,
Greet your sweetheart!"

Avdeeva, p. 116. The players move in a circle. One girl is inside the circle, and one boy is outside the circle. The song is a dialogue between the chorus and the boy. At the words: "Go, tsar, to the city"—the boy goes into the circle and kisses the girl-tsarevna (Propp).

51

Once in a city the tsaerevna, the tsarevna,
Once in a city the young girl, the young girl
In the middle of a circle stood, she stood,
Her precious ring she jangled, she jangled,
Her gold ring shone, it shone.

Once in a city the tsar's son, the tsar's son,
Once beyond the city he strolled, he strolled.
"Oh, sir, smash the gates, the gates.
Oh, sir, smash the second ones, the second,
Oh, sir, smash the third, yes, the third.
Oh, sir, enter the city, the city,
Go, sir, to the tsarevna, to the tsarevna,
Bow, sir, to the tsarevna, to the tsarevna,
Bow, sir, lower, lower,
And even lower, lower.
Take, sir, the tsarevna, the tsarevna,
By the right hand, her hand,
Oh, sir, kiss the tsarevna, the tsarevna,
Kiss her sweeter, sweeter,
So she be sweeter, sweeter."

What is our tsarevna like, our tsarevna?
What is our young girl like, our young girl?
She has a face so white, so white,
She has brows so black, so black.

Balakirev, no. 28. The girl tsarevna stands in the center of the circle, the boy tsar's son walks outside the xorovod opposite her. At the words: "Oh, sir, enter the city"—the boy enters the circle, stands opposite the tsarevna, bows to her and kisses her (Propp).

52

Mother wanted
To give me to Ivan,—
"I will not, I will not, mama,
I will not, I think not:
Ivan has a pit in his garden,
Forever there will I be."

Mother wanted
To give me to Stepan,—
"I will not, I will not, mama,
I will not, I think not:
Stepan has three glasses,
Forever will I be drunk."

Mother wanted
To give me to Philip,—
"I will not, I will not, mama,
I will not, I think not:
Philip has a linden in his garden,
Forever will I be beaten."

Mother wanted
To give me to a catkeeper,—
"I will not, I will not, mama,
I will not, I think not:
A catkeeper skins cats
And will keep my legs in check."

Mother wanted
To give me to a boyar,—
"I will not, I will not, mama,
I will not, I think not:
A boyar beats his peasants,
And I will have to beg for mercy.

Mother wanted
To give me to a clerk,—
"I will, I will, mama,
I will marry, I think so:
As the clerk writes
I will count his money."

Shein, no. 581. Transcribed 1864.

DISPERSAL SONGS

53

How should we begin our song,
How should we end it?
We shall begin with conversations,
We shall end with a kiss.

Shein, no. 478.

54

In a garden stands a little apple tree,
On it sits a nightingale,
Loudly it sings a little song,
It gives you no peace,
It is calling a maiden.
Where we will come together—we will bow,
We will disperse—we will say farewell.

Varencov, p. 128.

Wedding Songs

AT THE MARRIAGE CONTRACT

55

Bless you, Lord God,
Mother of God, Madonna!
They have sat me down, a young girl,
On a bench of beams,
They sing to me, a young girl,
A melancholy song.
Not with joy and gladness—
With grief and anguish,
With great sorrow,
With laments, with pity,
With burning tears.

Shein, no. 1467. The wailing songs of the bride begin with similar laments (Propp).

56

My provider, dear daddy!
Are you upset with me, are you bored with me,
Wasn't I a good servant to you?
Wasn't I an envoy for you?
Suddenly I have been driven from your warm nest,
No longer share your bread and salt,
No longer wear a pretty dress for you.
Wasn't I a good worker for you in the bare field,
A little cuckoo in your warm nest?

Shein, no. 2008. A lament addressed to the bride's father (Propp).

AT THE RUKOBIT'E

57

Oh mother of mine!
Cold winter will pass
Warm summer will come,

In the meadows green grass will grow,
Azure flowers will bloom,—
My girl friends will go,
My dear friends will go,
Dear friends, kind friends,
For a walk to the green meadows;
They will each cut a flower,
They will each weave a wreath.
My flower stands by the road,
Stands by the road, by the path:
No one will pluck it,
No one will weave a wreath,
It will dry up and fade—
My heart is aching
In a far-off land,
At a strange mother's and father's:
At a strange father's and mother's.
Conceited, arrogant, and proud,
They love conceit and big sticks
and low bows.
But I, bitter,
But I, full of grief,
Don't know how to submit to them,
Don't know how to bow down to them.
But at home, my own mother,
I was a tender child.
At home I knew neither conceit nor big sticks
Nor low bows.

Shein, no. 1607.

58

I spent the night, a young girl,
I spent the night sleeping little,
Many things did I see in my dreams.
There appeared to me, a young girl,
Many steep mountains,
Many quick rivers,
Many dark forests,
Many wild beasts.

What are the steep mountains—
My grief-sorrow,
What are the quick rivers—
My burning tears;

What are the dark forests—
A strange, far-off land,
What are the wild beasts—
Strange, unknown people.

Shein, no. 1361.

59

"Auntie, sweet dove!
Tell me, sweet dove,
How you parted
With your own daddy,
With your mama who nourished you,
With your dear falcon brother,
With your dear sister dove,
With your aunties and grandmas,
With your dove girl friends,
With kind, pretty girls,
With a maid's *krásota*,
With a maid's adornment?"

"I will tell you, little dove:
With difficulty I parted,
I parted, poor girl,
I left them, bitter!
I don't remember, a young girl,
Whether by my feet they dragged me out,
Whether in their arms they carried me out.
It is difficult to part
With your own daddy,
With your own mama,
With your kin-family;
How even more difficult
To part with a maid's *krásota*,
With a maid's adornment.
I will tell you even more, little dove,
About the strange far-off land,
About that cursed evil place.
It is difficult, my little dove,
Difficult to live in a strange land,
Difficult to live among strange people.
You must learn how to live,
You must understand how to speak.
You must call the old man uncle,
And call the old woman auntie,

You must extol the young ones by name,
By their patronymic.*
When my own mother
Would awaken me the first time—
She would stroke my head:
"Sleep, my dear child,
Sleep, my sweet one!"
And the second time she would awaken me—
She would wrap me in marten,
And the third time she would awaken me:
"Get up, my dear child!
I have done everything,
The work is done!"
Well, I'd get up, a young girl,
I'd wash with spring water,
I'd rub myself with a towel.
Everything was done,
All the work was done.
At my mother's,
At my father's
I didn't know, a young girl,
Where the sun rises
Where the beautiful sun sets.
In a strange land
I found out, a young girl,
Where the sun rises,
Where the beautiful sun sets.
In that strange land,
In that cursed, evil place
With a strange father and mother—
My strange mother walks
Along the creaking rooms of the shed,
Along the shaky passages:
"Get up, sleepy daughter-in-law,
You get up, drowsy daughter-in-law!
I've prepared everything,
All the work's ready to be done."
I get up, a young girl,
I wash myself with burning tears,
I dry myself with my sleeve.

Shein, nos. 1378, 1379.

*Patronymic—in Russian, a sign of respect, not used with relatives or children (Tr.).

AT THE DEVIČNIK

60

Thank you, dear mama,
Tender and kind!
You took care of me, mama,
In my long maidenhood,
You sheltered me, mama,
From people's disparaging words,
Every year, mama, you gave me
My freedom as a present.
And now they're taking my freedom away,
From me, a young girl,
Yes, and you yourself, mama,
Have given your consent.
Goodby, my darling,
Beloved little sun!
Bless me, mama,
Bless me, don't be angry,
Don't remember, dear one,
My girlish foolishness,
My unkind words!

Rybinkov, p. 61.

61

Lord Ermil strolls through the courtyard,
He chooses a good horse,
He fully equips himself
And rides up to his mother-in-law's courtyard:
"Mother-in-law, dear mother-in-law;
Let me into the courtyard,
Let me see my promised bride!
I have brought her a dress,
A dress of precious stones!"
"A dress she does not need,
But she needs something else!
She has a dress at home."

Lord Ermil strolls through the courtyard,
He chooses a good horse,
He fully equips himself
And rides up to his mother-in-law's courtyard:

"Mother-in-law, dear mother-in-law;
Let me into the courtyard,
Let me see my promised bride!
I have brought her pearls,
Pearls and diamonds,
Diamonds and rubies!"
"Pearls and diamonds
And rubies she does not need,
She needs something else!
She has all that at home."
Lord Ermil strolls through the courtyard,
He chooses a good horse,
He fully equips himself
And rides up to his mother-in-law's courtyard:
"Mother-in-law, dear mother-in-law;
Let me into the courtyard,
Let me see my promised bride!
I have brought a golden ring,
A golden ring with diamonds,
With diamonds and with rubies!"
"Well, sir, come in,
Please ride in to your promised bride,
To your betrothed!
She needs a golden ring,
She needs one with diamonds,
With diamonds and with rubies;
With this ring will she be married."

Kireevskij, n.s., issue I, no. 920.

ON THE DAY OF THE WEDDING

62

Say farewell, my dear girl friends,
My dear little doves,
If I was rude—don't be angry!
You, my darlings, will be off
To summer work,
For merry walks,
To winter parties,—
Remember me, my darlings,
In the spring, in the green meadows,
When you will be weaving wreaths

For me, for a pretty maid.
I don't need a pale blue wreath:
I wove one for the last time
And threw it into the rapid river,—
The wreath was carried off to a strange land,
To the blue sea of Svalynsk.

Shein, no. 2206. This is a farewell song of the bride before her departure (Propp).

63

Don't spill over, my quiet Danube,
Don't overflow green meadows!
In those meadows is feather-grass,
In that grass walks a white deer,
Walks a white deer—golden horns.
Ivan the lord rode by,
Spiridonovič* rode by,
And whipped the little deer with a lash.
"Don't beat me, Lord Ivan,
Don't beat me, Spiridonovič!
Someday I will prove useful to you:
You will marry—to the wedding will I come
The courtyard will I enter—the whole courtyard will
        I light up,
The chamber will I enter—all the guests will I cheer,
And most of all your Mar'ja,
So she will cry less,
So she won't grieve."

Kireevskij, n.s., vyp. I, no. 593.

64

You get up, mother of mine!
You slept through the dark night,
But I, a young girl, did not sleep,
This dream appeared to me:
I was walking along steep mountains,
I was collecting thick berries.
The steep mountains are my sorrow,
The thick berries are my tears.

Pomerenceva, II, p. 188. Transcribed 1924. This is the morning lament of the bride when she gets up (Propp).

*Ivan's patronymic

RITUAL BATH*

65

I could not wash away my grief,
I could not rinse away my tears
From my rosy face,
From a passionate, wishful heart.
I washed my little white hands,
I washed my little white breasts
Not under bright chains,
Not under yellow amber . . .

66

We, white swans, set out
For the hot steam bath
For your maiden *krásota*.
We opened the narrow doors,
Walked in quietly;
We took your maiden *krásota*
Wrapped it in a towel.
We, white swans, set out
Along the glorious wide street,
Along the public road.
A raging wind began to blow,
The towel waved about!
The maiden *krásota* flew away
Beyond the high mountains,
Beyond the deep swamps.
And your *krásota* settled
On the public road,
On a little white birch,
On a white, curly birch,
On the very top!

Kolpakova, p. 232.

---

*This and the following song were selected from N. P. Kolpakova, ed., *Lirika russkoj svad'by* [Lyrics of the Russian Wedding] (Leningrad, 1973), p. 231.

PRAISE SONGS

On an oak are two doves,
They sit, converse,
converse
And me, a young man, they praise:
"We have such a fantastic person among us
Like the wedding guest Ivan Stepanovich the merchant!"

Kolpakova, p. 181.

Good matchmaker
Good matchmaker
You're wearing a marten coat
You are wearing a marten coat
A beaver hat
A beaver hat,
And you're black-browed
You are black-browed.

Kolpakova, p. 173.

MOCKING SONGS

Tysjackij* so terrible
Tysjackij so terrible!
He was sitting on a horse from the vegetable garden
He on a horse is like a raven
And the horse under him is like a cow!

Kolpakova, p. 203.

*The tysjackij acts as the patron of the groom. He is often his godfather. See "Stravinsky's 'Les Noces,'" translated and with an Introduction by Roberta Reeder and Arthur Comegno, *Dance Research Journal* (Winter 1986–87): 31–63.

Vocal Songs About Family Life

67

My nightingale, little nightingale,
My nightingale, my own daddy!
Fly, my little nightingale,
To your native land,
And ask, little nightingale:
Who has the freedom, who hasn't the freedom to stroll?
"Pretty girls have the freedom,
Young married women have no freedom;
A young married woman
Has three great worries:
The first worry—
A strange far-off land;
The second worry—
A very difficult mother-in-law;
And the third worry—
A foolhardy husband!
My husband won't allow me out to stroll,
He orders me not to jump, not to dance,
Nor to play in the *xorovod* with young men,
But I must always sit with him, like with an idol,
Both day and night and keep spinning thread!"

Sobolevskij, II, no. 130.

68

Mama gave me in marriage in a far-off land;
Mama wanted to come often,
To come often, to stay a long time.
One summer passes—no mama;
Another passes—no lady;
The third is here—mama comes.
But mama no longer recognizes me:
"Who is this *baba*,* this old lady?"

* *baba*—an old peasant woman (Tr.).

"I'm not a *baba*, I'm not an old lady,
I'm your sweet child, mama."
"Where has your white body gone,
Where has your scarlet blush gone?"
"My white body—under a silken lash,
My scarlet blush—under his right hand:
With a lash he strikes—my body decreases;
My cheek he strikes—my blush disappears."

Čulkov, pt. I, no. 158 (Sobolevskij, III, no. 44).

69

In the green garden a pear tree
  Began to rustle, to rustle.
Why in the garden has the pear tree
  Begun to rustle, to rustle?
And the sharp, wild winds,
  Little winds begun to blow.
In Mixail's home there was joy,
  There was joy.
In Ivanovič's* home there was joy,
  There was joy.
Why in his home
  Was there joy, was there joy?
His young wife a son
  Has borne, has borne,
And the sweet Theodosia-darling a son
  Has borne, has borne,
Sweet Petrovna*—darling a son
  Has borne, has borne.

Avdeeva, p. 99.

70

Splinter,** little birchen splinter!
Oh, why, little splinter, aren't you burning bright?

---

*Ivanovič, Petrovna—in Russia, adults who are not relatives or close friends are addressed by their first name and patronymic, which is derived from the father's name: "—ovič" is added for a man, "—ovna" for a woman. In this case, Mixail's father's name was Ivan and Theodosia's father's name was Peter. Normally he would be called Mixail Ivanovič and she Theodosia Petrovna, but in this song their names are broken up, a division which often occurs in Russian folk lyrics (Tr.).

**Splinter [*lučina*]—used by peasants to furnish light, since they could not afford to use candles (Tr.).

Not burning, burning bright, not bursting into flame?
Was it, little splinter, that you weren't in the stove,
Or was it, little splinter, that you weren't dried out,
Or did my nasty mother-in-law pour water on you?

Girl friends-little doves, go to sleep!
Go to sleep, my friends, you have no one to wait for!
But for me, a young girl, there is no sleep the whole night!
The whole night no sleep for a young girl, but I must make
      the bed,
Make the bed and wait for my sweetheart!
The first dream I dreamt—my sweetheart is not here;
The second dream I dreamt—my darling is not here;
The third dream I dreamt—the white light of dawn!
In the white dawn walks my sweetheart:
His boots squeak,
His sable coat rustles,
And on his fur coat the buttons jingle.

71

Oh, my life, my life,
Life, bitter life,
You, my life, are a misfortune:
My husband is old, I am young.
He needs a *polati*,*
I want to take a walk,
To take a walk with a young man,
Not with an old gray-haired man.
It would be nothing,
His old age itself;
Old age wouldn't matter,—
But he is quarrelsome besides.
If only he were not quarrelsome!
He is jealous—a misfortune,
He never lets me out anywhere,
He locks the gate.
Still it is not really locked—
He locks the fence.
But the fence is nothing—
I will jump over, I will go over!

Eifmenko, p. 55 (Sobolevskij, II, no. 413).

*polati—a broad berth near the ceiling for sleeping (Tr.).

72

Oh, my winds, oh winds, you raging winds!
Oh, winds, can't you rock away my sorrow?
Oh, my gusli, oh gusli, sweet gusli,*
Oh, gusli, can't you bring a widow joy?
I, a widow, have four sorrows,
Four sorrows, and a fifth grief,
A fifth grief, and nothing could be greater!
The first sorrow—there is no firewood, no splinter;
The second sorrow—there is no bread, no salt;
The third sorrow—I became a widow young;
The fourth sorrow—there are many small children;
And the fifth grief—there is no master in the house.
I will sow grief in the bare field.
Go away, my grief, like black *černobyl'nik*,**
Like black *černobyl'nik*, like bitter wormwood.

Mordovceva and Kostomarov, p. 110 (Sobolevskij, II, no. 214).

73

Once in the glorious city of Čerkask
There new stone palaces were built;
In the palaces were standing strong oaken tables,
At the table was sitting a young widow,
Sitting by herself, crying tearfully,
In tears she laments,
Her ardent heart curses:
"Cursed is the ardent heart within me!
Enough of pain for you, my little heart!
It is time for you, my heart, to forget your beloved!
I will awaken from my dream, and will tell my fortune!
When my frisky legs will tire,
When my wild head will fall from my shoulders,
Then will I forget my dearly beloved."

Donskie oblastnye vedomosti, 1875, no. 87 (Sobolevskij, III, no. 213).

---

*gusli—a stringed instrument used by medieval Russian minstrels (Tr.).
**černobyl'nik—a variety of wormwood with reddish-brown or violet-brown stems (Tr.).

Xorovod, Game, and Dance Songs about Family Life

74

I will tell mama—
My head aches,
I feel bad,
I feel like taking a walk!
I'll sneak off—
I'll walk a bit,
I'll steal away—
I'll go kissing.
"Oh, you dear young man!
Teach me, sweetheart,
How to walk home."
"Walk, clever girl,
Walk, smart girl:
By a quick little street—
By a little gray duck,
Across the black dirt—
By a quail-hen,
To a wide courtyard—
By a pretty girl,
To a high tower—
By a young wife."
My high tower
Stands open.
All the windows
Are unfastened.
My hateful husband
Sits at the table,
Eating bread and salt.
"The bread and salt are for you,
My hateful husband!"
When my husband
Gets up,
He takes

A silken lash.
The silken lash
Whipped me,
And I, a young girl,
Yelled and cried.
I thought
And thought some more:
To whom
Could I pray?
I prayed
To my father-in-law:
"Father-in-law,
Take me away
From these beatings,
From these terrible beatings!"
My father-in-law
Was lying on the stove,
Was lying on the stove,
Growling like a dog,
He gave orders to have me beaten some more,
He gave orders to spill my blood.
I thought,
And thought some more:
To whom
Could I pray?
I prayed to my mother-in-law:
"Mother-in-law,
Take me away
From these beatings,
From these terrible beatings!"
My mother-in-law
Was lying on the stove,
Hissing like a snake,
She gave orders to have me beaten some more,
She gave orders to spill my blood.
I thought
And thought some more:
To whom
Could I pray?
"Oh, my dear
Kind husband!
Love me,
Don't beat me,

Don't beat me,
Kiss me instead!"

Shein, no. 463. "In singing this song, the girls form a circle, and one stands in the center and performs everything sung in the song" (Shein). See Sobolevskij, II, nos. 524–537 (Propp).

75

Last evening they deceived Dunja,
To an old man, to an old man they married her.
She lived not long with the old man,
In all only three days.
On the fourth day, on the fourth day she calls him
    to the field:
"Let's go, old man, let's go, old man, to the bare field!
In the bare field, in the bare field is a blue sea,
And on an island, and on an island a flower has bloomed,
Go, old man, go, old man, and pick the flower."
"I'm afraid, wife, I'm afraid, wife, that I'll drown!"
"It's most likely, old man, it's most likely, old man,
    the devil won't grab you."
The first step, the first step is up to his knees,
The second step, the second step came up to his waist,
The third step, the third step came up to his neck.
He cries: "Wife," he cried, "wife, I'm drowning!"
"Thank God, thank God, you're drowning,
Thank God you're drowning!"

Promeranceva I, no. 119. Every line is repeated (Propp).

76

"Well, tell me, wife,
And where, my wife, have you been?"
"I was, sir, I was
At the priest's visiting."
"Well, tell me, wife,
What did you eat and drink?"
"I drank, sir, I drank
A lot of beer and wine."
"Well, tell me, wife,
Did you remember me?"
"To your health, sir,
I drank a glass of *kvass*."*

---

* *kvass*—a Russian drink made from fermented rye, barley, and rye bread (Tr.).

"Just wait, wife,
I'm going to beat you!"
"And I'll pay you back twice,
I'll pay you back twice,
You old grumbler;
I'll swing my back sideways,
And find myself a young man,
A young one,
Yes, a young one,
And a handsome one,
A handsome one,
Yes, a bachelor."

Shein, no. 619.

Joking and Satirical Vocal Songs: *Xorovod*, Game, and Dance Songs

77

Oh, mama, I cannot,
Madame, I cannot,
A mosquito stepped on my foot,
It crushed my whole foot,
It hurt all my joints,
It hurt all my joints,
I've been lame for a week.

Gurevič and Èliasov, no. 160. Transcribed 1937.

78

On a mountain stood a monastery,
With an awful lot of monks.
They were all terrible drunkards,
They drank vodka from a phial.
And their abbot was an old man,
He ordered them to drink a lot of wine.
"Well, brothers, let's get raging mad,
Let's not go to evening mass or matins."
And he rolled them a barrel of white wine.
Let's drink our fill
And settle down to sleep behind the barrel."

Pomeranceva II, no. 29. Transcribed 1956. See Sobolevskij, VII, no. 345.

79

Along the cell I walk, and wake up the little nun:
"You, little nun, get up, little savior, get up,
They're ringing for vespers and the clocks are sounding,
People are gathering, they are praying to God!"
"I can't get up, raise my head:
My back aches, it won't let me kneel!"

Along the cell I walk, and wake up the little nun:
"You, little nun, get up, little savior, get up!
Musicians have come and they brought their fiddles!"
"Ah, I'll get up, I'll dance,
I'll break my bones, I'll make the guests merry!"

"You, little nun, are a sin, little savior, a sin!"
"I'll take my *golik** and sweep away the sins:
Under the bench are sins, and on the bench sins,
All around the cell are sins!"

Otečestvennye zapiski, 1858, no. 1, p. 329 (Sobolevskij, VII, p. 361). From a manuscript collection of the eighteenth century.

80

It was in the city of Kazan,
     Zduninaj-naj-naj, in Kazan,
A young monk was shorn.
The monk felt like taking a walk
Beyond the holy gates.
Beyond the gates was a *besedka*.**
In the *besedka* were some old peasant women.
But the monk won't look over there,
The monk pulls his cowl over his eyes.

It was in the city of Kazan,
A young monk was shorn.
The monk felt like taking a walk,
Beyond the holy gates.
Beyond the gates sat a *besedka*.
In the *besedka* were young married women.
Now the monk will take a look,
The monk will raise his cowl.

It was in the city of Kazan,
A young monk was shorn.
The monk felt like taking a walk,
Beyond the holy gates.
Beyond the gates was a *besedka*.
In the *besedka* were some pretty maids.

*golik—a broom of bare twigs (Tr.).

**besedka—a small park building for resting and for protection from the rain and sun (Tr.).

Well, now the monk will take a look,
The monk will throw off his cowl.
"Oh, burn, my boring cell,
Vanish, my black garment!
I, a young man, have had enough of being saved!
Isn't it time for me, a fine fellow, to marry
A sweet, pretty maid,
      Zduninaj-naj-naj, a maid?"

Prač, no. 128 (Sobolevskij, VII, no. 337). After every line there is a refrain with the repetition of the preceding half-line (Propp).

81

In the city of Rostov
At a fat boyar's
In a wide courtyard
Once lived two brothers,
Two sturdy fellows,
Erëma and Fomá.
They lived awfully well,
Drank, ate sweets,
Walked about in style.
Erëma ate horse-radish,
Fomá garlic,
Grief takes hold of Fomá,
Grief takes hold of Fomá.

"Haven't we had enough, dear brother,
Of eating sweets?
Let's go, dear brother,
And walk about in elegant style."
Erëma in a loose overall,
Fomá in a peasant's coat.
Grief takes hold of Fomá.
Grief takes hold of Fomá.

"Haven't we had enough, dear brother,
Of walking about in elegant style
And living at the lord's?
Let's go, dear brother,
And set up house."
Erëma bought an ax,
And Fomá a chisel,
Erëma's couldn't chop,
Fomá's was a failure,

Grief takes hold of Fomá,
Grief takes hold of Fomá.

"Haven't we had enough, dear brother,
Of setting up house?
Let us, dear brother,
Plough some land."
Erëma harnessed a cat,
And Fomá a rooster,
Erëma's wouldn't pull,
Fomá's wouldn't draw,
Grief takes hold of Fomá,
Grief takes hold of Fomá.

"Haven't we had enough, dear brother,
Of ploughing the field?
Let us, dear brother,
Sow rye."
Erëma sowed,
But Fomá didn't have time,
Grief takes hold of Fomá,
Grief takes hold of Fomá.

"Haven't we had enough, brother,
Of sowing rye?
Let us, brother
Harvest the rye."
Erëma took an awl,
And Fomá a curved awl.
Erëma's wouldn't cut,
Fomá's was a failure.
Grief takes hold of Fomá,
Grief takes hold of Fomá.

"Haven't we had enough, brother,
Of harvesting the rye?
Let us, brother,
Put it in a sheaf."
They put it in a sheaf
On the stove pipe,
The cat jumped,
And dropped the sheaf.

"Haven't we had enough, brother,
Of putting it into a sheaf?

Let us, dear brother,
Thresh the rye."
Erëma with his whip,
And Fomá with his fist.
Erëma's didn't sprinkle,
Fomá's didn't fly,
Grief takes Fomá,
Grief takes Fomá.

"Haven't we had enough, brother,
Of threshing the rye?
Let us, dear brother,
Soak the rye."
Erëma's turned sour,
Fomá's turned dank,
Grief takes Fomá,
Grief takes Fomá.

"Haven't we had enough, brother,
Of soaking the rye?
Let us, dear brother,
Sell the malt."
Erëma sold it,
Fomá gave it away,
Grief takes hold of Fomá,
Grief takes hold of Fomá.

"Haven't we had enough, brother,
Of bargaining,
Of bringing in a profit?
Let us, dear brother,
Go hunting,
To catch rabbits."
Erëma with a cat,
And Fomá with a rooster.
Erëma's didn't catch,
Fomá's didn't run,
Grief takes Fomá,
Grief takes Fomá.

"Haven't we had enough, brother,
Of going hunting,
To catch rabbits?
Let us, dear brother,
Go to church."

Erëma went to church,
Fomá went up to the altar,
Erëma began to sing,
Fomá began to roar.
The stern sexton came up,
Grabbed Fomá by the neck,
Grief takes Fomá,
Grief takes Fomá.

"Haven't you had enough, brother,
Of going to church
And praying to God?
Let us, dear brother,
Go fishing."
Erëma bought a net,
Fomá a snare,
Erëma bought a boat,
Fomá a little boat.
The large boat was fragile,
And the little boat without a bottom.

Erëma covered his,
And Fomá also covered his.
Erëma said:
"We'll be back by St. Peter's Day."
And Fomá said:
"As the Lord commands us."
Erëma dangled,
And Fomá stumbled.
Erëma fell into the water,
Fomá went to the bottom,
From Erëma came waves,
And from Fomá bubbles,
memory of Erëma they made pancakes,
In memory of Fomá they made pies.*

A. M. Smirnov, no. 145. Transcribed 1847. See Sobolevskij, VII, nos. 1–15.

*In his discussion of parellelism in poetry, "Poèzija grammatiki i grammatika poèzii" [The Poetry of Grammar and the Grammar of Poetry], *Poetics* (The Hague, 1961), p.401, Roman Jakobson discusses one stanza of this song. He shows that the paired phrases in this lyric are only apparently different; they actually show tautological characterisitics by means of synonymous expressions or parallel references to similar phenomena. He uses an example from a variant of the lyric: "Erëma ušël v bereznik, a Fomá v dubnik" [Erëma went into a birch forest, and Fomá into an oak forest]. "The difference between the juxtaposed actions of the two brothers lacks any significance; the elliptical phrase "Fomá into an oak forest" is an exact repetition of the phrase "Erëma went into a birch forest";

82

Once upon a time lived Dunja,
Dunja the fine-spinner.
          Pile it up, pile it up, Dunja,
          Dunja the fine-spinner!
Our Dunja spun
Neither thick nor thin,
Neither thick nor thin,
But a slightly thick rope,
A slightly thick rope,
And slightly thick shafts.
Our Dunja began
To warp the cloth.*
She warped and warped—
She broke her stake.
Our Dunja began
To weave linen.
Seven villages she passed,
And didn't find a loom reed.**
In the kitchen garden she wove,
And beat† with a stake.
Boyars rode up,
"God help us," they said,
"God help us," they said,
You've woven a bast mat."
"Your mug is lying,
This is not a bast mat,
This is not a bast mat—
It's fine linen.
Our Dunja began
To cut out a shirt:
With a chisel she measures,
With a butt she hits it.
Our Dunja began

---

both heroes, however, ran into the forest, and if one preferred the birch and the other the oak, it is only because Erëma and beréznik [birch forest] are exact amphibrachs, and Fomá and dubnik are both iambs." Jakobson points out that not only the brothers but everything surrounding them are described in synonym parallelism (Tr.).

*warp—to prepare the yarn for weaving (Tr.).

**loom reed—a device on a loom. It is used to draw threads between the separated threads of the warp (Tr.).

†beat—beating, or pushing the pick a certain distance away from the last one inserted, is necessary, since it is impossible to lay the weft close to the junction of the warp and the cloth already woven (Tr.).

To sew the shirt:
With a gimlet* she twists,
With a rope she pulls.
They began to put
The shirt on Dunja:
Seven held her,
Nine dressed her.
For seven years she wore it—
Did not ask for a change,
Did not ask for a change,
Did not go to the bathhouse.
Pile it up, pile it up, Dunja,
Dunja fine-spinner!

Novikova, p. 327. Transcribed 1936. The refrain is repeated every two lines. See Sobolevskij, VII, nos. 17–21.

83

"Tell us, tell us, little sparrow,
Tell us, tell us, young one,
How do old people walk,
How do they stroll?"
"They go this way, and that way,
And they all go this way!"

"Tell us, tell us, little sparrow,
Tell us, tell us, young one,
How do young men walk,
How do they stroll?"
"They go this way, and that way,
And they all go this way!"

"Tell us, tell us, little sparrow,
Tell us, tell us, young one,
How do young married women walk,
How do they stroll?"
"They go this way, and that way,
And they all go this way!"

"Tell us, tell us, little sparrow,
Tell us, tell us, young one,
How do young maids walk,

---

*gimlet—a boring tool (Tr.).

How do they stroll?"
"They go this way and that way,
And all go this way!"

"Tell us, tell us, little sparrow,
Tell us, tell us, young one,
How do priests walk,
How do they stroll?"
"They go this way and that way,
And all go this way!"

"Tell us, tell us, little sparrow,
Tell us, tell us, young one,
How do their wives walk,
How do their wives stroll?"
"They go this way and that way,
And all go this way!"

Možarvoskij, p. 75 (Sobolevskij, VII, no. 580). Each line of the answer is repeated (Propp).

Children's Songs

LULLABY

84

The cat, the cat
Has a golden cradle,
But my little child
Has a better one:
A finely made cradle
Golden!
The cat, the cat
Has a white pillow,
My child
Has a whiter one.
The cat, the cat
Has a soft bed,
My child
Has a softer one.

Kireevskij, n.s., issue I, no. 1104.

SONGS BY CHILDREN

85

"Kisan'ka! Where have you been?"
"At the mill."
"What did you do?"
"Ground flour."
"How much did you earn?"
"A grosh."
"What did you buy?"
"A *kalačik*."*
"Who did you eat it with?"
"Alone."

Shein, no. 63.

* *kalačik*—a type of fancy bread.

86

Knocking-banging down the street,
Foma is riding on a hen,
Timoška on a cat
There down the road.
"Foma, where are you riding,
Where are you rushing?"
"To mow the hay."
"Why do you need hay?"
"To feed the cows."
"Why do you need cows?"
"To milk."
"Why do you need milk?"
"To give to my children to drink."

Shein, no. 104.

Barge Hauler Songs

87

Leader

Cudgel, little cudgel,
Oh, cudgel of green,
Of green, let's pull!

Chorus

Let's pull!
Let's pull!
There it went! There it went!
It went by itself, it went by itself!

Leader

Oj ljuli! Oj ljuli!
The bark stayed on the shoal.
Well, let's pull!

Chorus

Let's pull!
Let's pull!
There it went! There it went!
It went by itself, it went by itself!

Leader

Eh, on the river, in the meadow,
Eh, let's pull, let's pull,
Well, come on, let's pull!

Chorus

Let's pull!
Let's pull!
There it went! There it went!

It went by itself, it went by itself!

Leader

Eh, pull, pull until we sweat,
A grosh will be added to the price of work.

Chorus

Let's pull!
Let's pull!
There it went! There it went!
It went by itself, it went by itself!

Tonkov, p. 71, no. 17. Transcribed from Don barge haulers.

88

Eh, uxnem! Eh, uxnem!
Once more, once again!
Eh, uxnem! Eh, uxnem!
Once more, once again.

We will swing the birch!
We will toss the curly birch!
Aj-da, da, aj-da, aj-da, da, aj-da,
We will toss the curly birch!

Balakirev, no. 36.

Robber Songs

89

Down along the Mother Volga
Along the wide expanse,

Along the wide expanse
Arose a storm, bad weather.

Arose a storm, bad weather,
A great storm,

A great storm,
Great waves,

Great waves,
Nothing can be seen in the waves,

Nothing can be seen in the waves,
Only a pretty boat can be seen.

Only a pretty boat can be seen.
A pretty red boat,

A pretty red boat,
Black caps on the rowers,

Black caps on the rowers,
The captain himself is well dressed,

The captain himself is well dressed,
In a brown robe,

In a brown robe,
"Head, fellows,

"Head, fellows,
For the steep shore,

For the steep shore,
For the yellow sand."

Lopatin and Prokunin, no. 74; see Sobolevskij, II, no. 552. The song usually continues
further: the rowers come up to the shore and are met by a girl. In the folk drama *Lodka*
[The Boat], this song is sung by robbers (Propp).

90

It happened below the city of Saratov,
It happened above the city of Tsaritsyn,
The river Mother Kamyšenka flowed by,
And behind it ran steep shores,
Steep-beautiful shores, green meadows,
At its mouth it fell into the Mother Volga.
Along that river Mother Kamyšenka
Sail the Cossack captain's boats,
On these boats sit the oarsmen,
All are barge haulers, all are young men of the Volga.
All the brave young men were dressed up:
They wore caps of sable, tops of velvet;
They wore damask *odnorjadka** kaftans;
Hemp quilted jackets stitched in thread,
Silken shirts edged with gold lace,
All the young men wore boots of Moroccan leather.
With their oars they rowed and sang songs.
Near an island in the midst of the Volga they stopped:
They waited and waited for the governor,
For the Astrakhan governor they waited.
And the brave barge haulers speak:
"Isn't that something white nearby on the water?
The white flags of the governor:
Whoever we were waiting for will get it."
The Astrakhan governor was suspicious:
"Oh, you're barge haulers, free people!
Take all the golden treasure you need,
Take the governor's colored gown,
Take all the foreign wonders,
Take all the Astrakhan knick-knacks!"
Then the brave, free men replied:
"But we don't value your golden treasure,
We don't value your governor's gown,
We don't value foreign wonders,
We don't value Astrakhan knick-knacks—

odnorjadka—a single-breasted kaftan without a collar (Tr.).

What we value is your wild head."
They cut off the governor's wild head,
They threw the head into the Mother Volga,
The young men laughed at him:
"You well know, governor, you have been harsh toward us,
You beat us, you destroyed us, sent us into exile,
Shot our wives and children at the gates!"

Kireevskij, VII, p. 149. Similar songs exist about the killing of the princes Karamyšev, Repnin, Gagarin, and Golicyn (Propp).

91

Do not rustle, mother green oak grove,
Do not keep me, a fine young man,
　　　　from thinking about things!
Tomorrow they will take me, a fine young man,
　　　　to be questioned,
Before a terrible judge—the tsar himself.
And the Lord-Tsar will begin to ask:
"Tell me, tell me, child, peasant's son,
With whom have you stolen, with whom have you robbed,
Were there many comrades with you?"
"I will tell you, my hope, Orthodox tsar,
The whole truth will I tell you, the whole truth.
There were four comrades with me:
My first comrade was the dark night;
And my second comrade was a steel knife;
And my third comrade was my good horse;
My fourth comrade was my taut bow;
My messengers were red-hot arrows."
And hope, the Orthodox tsar said:
"Glory to you, child, peasant's son,
That you knew how to steal, knew how to answer!
For this, child, will I reward you
With a tall mansion in the midst of a field
With two pillars and a crossbeam."

Čulkov, pt. I, no. 13 (Sobolevskij, VI, no. 424).

92

"Orphan, little orphan, bitter orphan,
Orphan, so bitter, so wretched,
Sing away your sorrow, orphan, with a song."
"It's all right for you, brothers, to sing—you have dined,

But I, an orphan, lay down without supper,
Lay down without supper, got up without breakfast.
I, an orphan, have neither bread nor salt,
No, neither bread nor salt, no, nor sour šči,*
One crust of dried bread, and that's from the summer."
"Tell us, tell us, orphan, who bore you?"
"My own mama bore me, an orphan,
I was nursed and fed by Mother Volga,
I was brought up by a light boat of white willow,
I was rocked by nana and mama, the fast waves,
I was raised by the strange far-off land of Astraxan,
And from this land I went to become a robber."
"Tell us, tell us, orphan, with whom did you steal?"
"Not all alone did I steal, with three comrades:
My first comrade was the dark night,
My second comrade was my steed, a good horse,
My third comrade was a steel rifle."

Mordovceva and Kostomarov, p. 76 (Sobolevskij, VI, no. 394).

---

* šči—cabbage soup (Tr.).

Soldier Songs

93

There was once a rich peasant
Who had three good sons.
But misfortune befell them—
Slavery—recruiting!
It would have been a pity to give away the oldest son,
And he didn't feel like giving away the middle one;
Should the youngest son go or not.
And the youngest son cried:
"Oh, and am I not your very own son?"
And the father said:
"Ah, indeed, you're my very own children,
Ah, go into the green garden
And cut off lots,
And throw the lots!"
And the oldest son got it.
The oldest son became sad,
His young wife cried,
The little children sobbed.
Then the smallest son said:
"Oh, don't cry, my kin:
I will go for you willingly."

Jakuškin, p. 555 (Sobolevskij, VI, no. 87).

94

How is our glorious land being ploughed?
Not by wooden ploughs is our glorious land being
        ploughed, not by iron ploughs—
Our land is being ploughed by horses' hooves;
And the glorious land is being sown with Cossack heads.
How is our glorious father the quiet Don adorned?
Our quiet Don is adorned with young widows.
How does our father the glorious quiet Don blossom?
Our father the glorious quiet Don blossoms with orphans.
What are the waves of the glorious quiet Don filled with?
The waves of the quiet Don are filled with fathers' and
        mothers' tears.

Pivovarov, p. 108 (Sobolevskij, VI, no. 3).

95

No longer, you winds of mine, little winds,
Fine little voices,
Do you blow in the forest,
Do you blow in the pine forest:
And the pine stands so wretched,
Stands so wretched, stands so melancholy!
The pines are standing on the river's edge,
On the steep shore;
Over the water rises the pine—
An ermine runs up to the pine,
Eats up its evil roots.
From the top of the pine bend its twigs,
Towards this pine bees are twisting,
They twist and keep twisting;
They bend toward it, and keep bending,
A young man's curls are twisting;
Grief-woe overtakes the young man:
They are giving him away to be a soldier!

Leopol'dov, p. 78 (Sobolevskij, VI, no. 23).

96

Along the mountains,
Along the high mountains
A young gray eagle
Was flying high
Flying high,
Shrieking pitifully.
In the formation a soldier
Was sighing heavily:
"For myself am I not sorry, not sorry
For myself,
I am only sorry
For the green garden:
In the green garden
Are three trees:
The first tree
Is a cypress,
The second tree
Is a sweet apple tree,
The third tree
Is a green pear tree.
The cypress tree

Is my dear daddy:
The sweet apple
Is my dear mamma,
The green pear
Is my young wife.

Maksimov, I, p. 403.

97

"Oh, field of mine, bare field,
Wide open spaces, so wide,

Wide open spaces, so wide.
How, little field, are you adorned?"

"I, a little field, am adorned with flowers,
With flowers, with cornflowers!"

Amidst the field is a thick willow bush,
Under the bush lies a white body.

Under the bush lies a white body,
A white body, a young soldier.

The young soldier lies, unslain,
Unslain he lies, but wounded badly.

In his head is a white-burning stone,
In his hand a sharp sword,

In his hands a sharp sword,
In his chest a fast bullet,

In his chest a fast bullet,
By his legs stands his good horse.

"Well, my horse, my horse, my comrade,
Go the the Russian land;

You tell, tell my dear daddy,
Bow down to my dear mama,

Bow down to my dear mama,
Tell, oh tell my young wife,

That I have married another wife,
I was married off to a white burning stone,

I was married off to a white burning stone,
A sharp sword married me off,

A sharp sword married me off,
My young wife—is a fast bullet."

Balakirev, no. 25. See Sobolevskij, I, no. 385-392.

98

It is not a little white birch bending toward the earth,
It is not silken grass spreading out in the field—
It is bitter wormwood spreading out, spreading out.
Nothing in the field is more bitter than you, wormwood!
More bitter than you, wormwood, is the Tsar's service,
Our military service,
For the white Tsar Peter the First!
Not during the day, but in the evening we soldiers
          clean our weapons;
At midnight the soldiers comb their hair,
Comb their hair and powder their curls;
In the white world the soldiers go on campaigns,
Go on campaigns, stand in formation,
Stand in formation and hold their rifles.
Stand with frisky feet in the damp earth,
Hold onto their fiery rifles with their white hands,
With their bright eyes they look beyond the Danube.
We have waited and waited for the enemy,
The enemy, the adversary—the Swedish king.
Our Swedish king came out of a white tent;
He looked at the Russian army out of a clear glass,
What kind of Russian army stands in formation,
In formation it stands holding its weapons.

Transcribed by the Ural Society of Lovers of Natural Science, VII, p. 124 (Sobolevskij, VI,
no. 192).

99

My nights so dark, my evenings so merry!
I sit for whole nights,
I turn over my thoughts;
One thought will not leave me:
If I had gray wings,

If I had golden feathers,
I would fly about, I would fly high,
I would fly far,
I would fly to my own land,
I would sit in my wide courtyard
I would look at, I would glance
At my high tower.
In that tower stand three tables.
At the first table sits my dear daddy,
At the second table my dear mama,
At the third table my young wife
With the small children.
Children of mine, orphaned children,
You still have no real daddy!

Varencov, p. 184 (Sobolevskij, VI, no. 232).

100

In the field the wind is blowing,
Soldiers are walking,
They're carrying a comrade
In a dirty overcoat.
They're carrying him to the train station,
To a cold car,
To Russia they are sending him
So he may be treated,
Treated or not—
We have sacrificed ourselves.
You take us into the infirmaries
Only to drive us into battle again.
It would be better for me to perish
In a distant land,
Don't let my relatives wait,
They'll forget about me.
In the field the wind is blowing,
Troops of soldiers are walking,
They're all in the trenches,
They will die as cripples.
The tsars, merchants, noblemen,
Are at tea drinking vodka,
But the poor soldiers
Are dying in the trenches for them.
The tsars, merchants, noblemen,
Gorge themselves full of bread,
But the poor soldiers

Are dying of hunger.
The soldiers defend
The lands of the rich.
But they take walks with the tsar
Under the roofs of churches.
In the field the wind is blowing,
Troops of soldiers are walking.
But a time will come
And the rich will be grabbed by the collar.

Birjukov, I, no. 27.

Songs of Prison, Penal Servitude, and Exile

101

Ah, why, my gray dove,
Ah, why won't you fly to me?
Do the frequent rains soak your wings,
Or raging winds carry you away?
Ah, why, my dear little friend,
Ah, why won't you come to me?
Won't your father or mother let you?
Does your family forbid you to love?
I will soon hear: my sweetheart is in captivity,
He is sitting in the city prison,
I will take golden keys
And unlock the coffers,
I will take 40,000 of the treasure,
I will ransom my sweetheart.
The judges do not wish to take the treasure,
They will not free my sweetheart.

Kašin, bk. 1, no. 18 (Sobolevskij, VI, no. 501).

102

You evil, malicious, nasty snake!
Out of your burrow, snake, you crawl and look around;
Along the sand, snake, you crawl and coil;
Along the grass, snake, you crawl and cause all the grass to
    wither,
All the azure flowers of the field have you caused to wither!
But, brothers, this is not a nasty, evil snake,
This, brothers, is an evil, beautiful maiden;
She led me, a fine young fellow, to ruin,
To an evil dark prison.

From the general headquarters in Moscow,
From the glorious Preobražen village
They are leading a fine young fellow to be executed and hanged.

Before the fine young fellow walks the Orthodox tsar;
To the right of the fine young fellow his father and mother;
To the left of the fine young fellow the terrible executioner;
Behind the fine young fellow walks the beautiful maiden.

Sobolevskij, VI, no. 461. Taken by Sobolevskij from a manuscript collection of the eighteenth century. Every line is repeated (Propp).

103

Gray hair of mine, dear gray hair,
My valiant gray hair,
Why have you appeared so early,
Why have you settled in my black curls?
Ah, you, my youth, oh, youth,
Ah, you, my fine youth!
I did not expect to waste you;
Ah, I wasted my youth,
Not in life, in wealth—
But in cursed loneliness!
I, a fine young fellow, have walked
From river mouths to mountain peaks
Walked over the whole Siberian land;
I, a fine young fellow, found
Neither father nor mother,
Neither brothers bright falcons,
Nor sisters, white swans;
But I, a fine young fellow, found
A captive, a beautiful young girl.

Finskij vestnik, 1847, no. 7 p. 24 (Sobolevskij, VI, no. 12). S. Maksimov in his book *Sibir'i Katorga* [Siberia and penal servitude] (1871, p. 272) says he heard this song in prisons from the prisoners (Propp).

104

A falcon had a little time:
The falcon flew high,
High he flew along the heavens;
He killed and kept killing the geese-swans,
The geese-swans, black ducks.
But now the falcon has no time:
The falcon sits in captivity,
In that golden cage,
Sits on a silver perch,
His lively feet enmeshed.

Maksimov, I, p. 109.

105

Without seeing each other, brothers, we took our leave,
From the white stone prison.
No longer in it shall we sit,
Soon we will set out on a long journey.
soon they will drive us to Siberia,
We will not be melancholy:
We will not spend time in Siberia,
We will not look into her eyes.
Here the road is large,
And it is possible to escape from the journey.
A tree stands near the road,
In the area of Samar-kabak.
We know the innkeeper,
He is one of us, one of the tramps;
For half a bottle of wine
Just pay him some money—
He'll take the shackles off us,
We'll be able to flee.
The executioner Fed'ka runs up,
He tears my shirt,
Puts me on the machine.
They put me on the machine,
Bind my arms and legs
With a raw leather strap.
Fed'ka takes the knout in his hand,
He cries out: "Brother, take care!"
He hits me the first time—
Tears poured out of my eyes;
He hit me a second time—
I cried: "Have mercy upon us!"

Mordovcev, p. 190 (Sobolevskij, VI, no. 531).

106

You tramps, you tramps,
    You dear tramps of mine!
You've had enough, you tramps,
    You've had enough of grief and sorrow;
Here comes winter-frost,
    We've been deprived of carousing.
The garrison stands in order,
    Drums at their side,

The drummers beat,
    They strike our rifle butts,
Shoulders, our backs they beat,
    They'll take us to the hospital.
They take off our shoes, undress us,
    Put us on cots,
With wet rags they wrap us,
    It seems they want to cure us.
We get up from the cots,
    Stand in a circle;
We look at each other—
    They begin to select us for work:
Who would go to the Bobrucka,
    Who to the Nerčinskij factory.
We're not afraid of Bobrucka,
    But we won't spend time in Nerčinskij:
The road there is long,
    We can escape off the road.
There is a village in the forest nearby,
    On the road stands a tavern,
We know the innkeeper,
    He is one of us, one of the tramps.
We'll get lots of wine,
    Make the supervisors drunk;
And the whole escort will get drunk
    And then we'll set out on a march.
We'll tie up the whole escort,
    Beat up the sentries,
We'll grab the weapons,
    And make off with them into the forest.

Maksimov, I, p. 426. See Sobolevskij, VI, no. 535.

Why, poor little boy,
Did you run off to your own land?
You asked for no one
Except your sweetheart.
Before, you used to drink, be merry,
When you had some money,
You went around with your comrades—
You squandered your money,
Your money disappeared—
You fell into a life of slavery,

Into such slavery—
Into the white stone prison.
It is hard being in slavery,
But who knows about it?
They put us in for a week—
We stayed a whole year.
We're behind three walls
We haven't seen the bright day;
But perhaps the Lord Creator is with us!
Bright stars shone for us in the night,
Even here we saw the dawn,
Even here we will not perish!
The bright stars have gone out,
The white dawn has appeared,
When the dawn has appeared,
A drum beat for the dawn.
A drum beat,
The watchman opened the door.
The watchman opened the door,
An officer comes with an order,
He calls each of us by name:
"Lads, put on
Your gray overcoats,
Take your small bags, knapsacks,
Come down below,
And everyone say something!"
What kind of fool's carriage
Appeared in the city?
They harness a pair of horses,
Drive this carriage,
Drive it up now.
To the main entrance;
They seat me, poor little boy,
Put me in backwards;
They take this poor little boy
Up to the scaffold pillar.
The executioneer Fed'ka runs up,
He takes me by the hand,
Takes me, a poor little boy,
By the funeral pillar.
They order me, a poor little boy,
To pray at sunrise,
To say farewell to the whole world.

107

The sun rises and sets,
But in my prison it is dark.
Day and night sentries
Keep my window under guard.

Since you want to keep guard,
I will not run away,
Although I want my freedom,
I cannot break my chains.

Ax, you chains, my chains,
You iron guards,
I cannot break you, cut you
Without a sharp knife.

I cannot stroll, as I used to,
During the dark night along the forests,
My youth has faded
In jails and in prisons.

Black raven, black raven,
Why are you soaring above me?
Or do you scent booty?
Black raven, I am not yours.

Novikova, p. 433. After the first performance of Maxim Gorky's play, *Na dne* [*Lower Depths*], which included this song, it became international and numerous variants were produced. It was widely sung in 1905 (Propp).

WORKER SONGS

108

Near, near a little city,
Near a little green garden,
Near a green garden,
Near the town of Yaroslavl',
Not far from a river,
Not far from a peasant village,
On a pretty, beautiful mountain,
On a high mountain,
On a high mountain,
Stood a large factory.
In that factory are young men—
Brave youths,
Brave young.
Not married, bachelors.
The young men from that factory
Gathered for a walk
To the pretty, the beautiful,
To the high mountain;
They sat along the edge,
Near the green garden,
Near the green garden,
Near the city of Yaroslavl';
They sat down, sang songs,
And ordered the nightingales to whistle:
"Nightingales, whistle!
We have come to walk among you!"
The nightingales whistled,
They comforted all the young men.
With us young men,
In Yaroslavl' city,
In Yaroslavl' city,
In Tolčkov district
At a soldier's widow's,
At a soldier's widow's,
Were some nice girls,
Some nice girls,
And Vasil'juška was there,
A master of carpet weaving;
Carpets he makes and weaves;
And he collects recruits:
He writes letters well,
He reads documents, too.

When he is in company
He plays the fiddle.
They played on the fiddle
For the soul of a pretty maid,
For the schooled, pretentious
Widow's daughter Pašenka.
The mother spoke to Paša,
And her brother tried to persuade her:
"Enough, Pašenka, stop,
Don't go out with young men!
These fellows will lead you
To ill fame!"
"Even if it leads me to ill fame,
I'll go out with them all."

Novyj rossijskij pesennik [New Russian Songbook], pt. 3 (St. Petersburg, 1791), p. 33 (Sobolevskij, VI, no. 533). Apparently the song consists of two songs; however, we know of such combinations in other variants (Propp).

109

To sort ore they have sent us
They keep flogging and abusing us,
They themselves not knowing—for what,
Far away they have sent us.
Let's go to Bel'mesova—
Let's sing a merry song,
Let's go to Šadrino—
Let's pester the foreman;
Let's go to Sauška—
We will ask an old lady
For drink, for food
And a place to sleep.
In the morning we'll get up,
Get our purses,
Eat dried crust,
And look into the distance.
We will see on the little mountain, on the mountain,
High and steep,
Over a dam, over the water
Stands the mine Golden Snake,*
But we hate it.
Our mining work
Gives us troubles.

*Golden Snake—the Zmeinogorsk mine was referred to as "golden-snaked" (Tr.).

At the place where they pan gold
Is a nasty supervisor.
He walks around, he stares at us,
Forces us to work,
Walks along hitting us with birch rods
And tears our hair out;
On holidays he keeps us working
And he himself doesn't know—for what.
We don't know who to complain to,
Only to God above;
But He is high above us,
And the tsar is so far away,
And we say: oh, oh,
Life is hard for us;
We live in barracks,
We eat only bread and water;
We will run away,
For whole days we will lie in the bushes;
But they will catch us,
And then flog us and work us to death.

V. Semevskij, "Iz istorii objazatel'nogo gornogo truda" [From a History of Obligatory Mountain Labor], *Sibirskij sbornik* [Siberian Collection], II, issue 1–2 (Irkutsk, 1897), pp. 47–49.

110

A seventeen-year-old boy
Decided in Petersburg to live.
In Petersburg there's lots of money,
Only they don't give it away!
He hadn't lived there three years
When he had to go home.
I'll go live in the village,
Just to get some money.
I had a reckoning with my master;
I didn't get a grosh!
With my fist I wiped away my tears,
I flew off on a distant journey.
As I traveled the long way
I lamented over my accounts;
Nine days and then on the tenth
I came to live in the village.
I arrived all ragged,
Everyone laughed at me:
"It's impossible to believe
That you haven't brought any money!

In Petersburg there's lots of money,
Only they don't give it away!
There are lots of wineshops, taverns—
But tea is better for you!
Live with us in the village,
Eat gray cabbage soup;
Live with us in the village,
Help us pull up stumps in the forest!"
The boy hadn't spent a year,
When he said farewell for Petersburg:
"I am going to live in Petersburg,
I'm going to save my money:
When I get a penny,
I'll put it in my trunk;
I'll collect a lot of money,
I'll take it all to a tavern;
Half the way we'll walk,
And the other half we'll ride
The other half we'll ride
And give it to the girls!"

V. Aleksandrov, "Derevenskoe vesel'e v Vologodskom uezde: Ětnografičeskie materialy" [Village Merry-making in the Vologod District: Ethnographic Material], *Sovremennik* [The Contemporary], no. 7 (1864), p. 172 (Sobolevskij, VI, no. 552).

III

In the Nižnetagil' factory,
Above a large old mine,
A fatal calamity befell
A young pauper;
At that time the owners' paws,
Like claws, held us all,
But Važgin, an artel member, seized everything,
Not thinking this a sin.
He took our money and bread
And tiny grains of sugar;
With our blood money
He built himself a house,
He built himself a tower
Out of large red bricks.
Every one of us was poor
And worked for him for many nights.
Važgin, on the order of Pavluxa,
Entered each of our houses
And drove each of us to work

With a big horse-whipping knout.
And for the time being we all
Had to submit to him
And everybody went to work
All year from dawn to dawn.

But the time came—and there appeared
Among us that brave pauper,
He never prayed to God,
And to us he talked like this:
"Comrades, my own brothers,
You've had enough of breaking your backs
So that your master-devils
Can rest on your labors.
The unhappy time has passed,
Pavluxa will not rule forever,
We will obtain justice ourselves
And won't work for the lords!"

He spoke, but Pavluxa
And with him the blood-sucker Važgin
Called up fifty Cossacks,
And there was only one command for them:
"Shoot, don't spare your cartridges,
If they go against us!"
They issued the order,
The Cossack sergeant gave them the order,
And the young pauper
They fettered in shackles
And, not allowing him to bid his family farewell,
They led him along the prison wall.
From the factory along the *ètap**
They drove him away quickly to Bajkal,
And the pauper died there unknown
Among those joyless cliffs.
But at home remained his father
And his old, decrepit mother.
And we will remember him together, fellows,
In peace.

Kaševarov and K. V. Bogoljubov, pp. 17–19. Pavluxa is the nickname of a factory owner, Demidov-San Donato, one of the descendants of the factory owners, the Demidovs, of the eighteenth century. The artel member Važgin really existed (Propp).

*ètap—a halting place for transported convicts (Tr.).

112

Peasants, you peasants,
In a word—fools!
You haven't been in the mines—
You haven't seen need and sorrow.

You haven't been in the mines
You haven't seen need and sorrow,
Come to the mines with us
You'll find out all about it.

Come to the mines with us,
You'll find out all about it,
You'll find out all about it,
About the life of the miner.

The miner doesn't plough the land,
He doesn't take a scythe in hand,
Doesn't take a scythe in hand,
Doesn't put money into the coffer.

Doesn't take a scythe in hand,
Doesn't put money into the coffer.
The miner knows cold, the miner knows hunger,
But neither bread nor water.

For the miner—cold, for the miner—hunger,
But neither bread nor water,
Neither bread nor water,
No freedom anywhere.

Birjukov, I, p. 281. The song is analogous to antiserfdom songs about the quarrel between the peasants and house serfs (Propp).

113

You, my forests, little forests, my dark forests!
You, my bushes, little bushes, broom bushes!
Why, little bushes, are you all broken?
The young factory men's eyes are full of tears,
On meeting them, the factory workers, the head bosses,
The head bosses of Grač and Skarnouxov* say:

*The Gračevs and Skarnouxovs were important manufacturers in the Moscow area at the end of the eighteenth and beginning of the nineteenth centuries (Tr.).

"Don't grieve, young men, young factory workers!
Young men, I will give you two new parlors,
Fancy wallpaper and good foundations,
And, young men, I will give you high pay,
High pay, napkins worth a ruble."

Kireevskij, n.s., issue 2, pt. 1, no. 1578.

114

Whoever has freedom, whoever has none,
No one knows my sorrow.
My sorrow is small,
Only it is inhuman.
My feet keep walking far,
My hands keep working hard.
Oh, I will go into the cherry orchard,
I will not pick berries,
Berries will I not pick,
I will only ask a nightingale:
"Gray-winged nightingale,
Tell me the truth, where is my sweetheart?"
"Oh, your sweetheart is at work,
At work in the sugar factory,
Oh, he works and works,
Ah, the sweat pours into his eyes.
The owner comes, scolds and chides him:
"Why, boy, have you made so many scraps,
Made so many scraps, broken the pipes,
Steam is spreading all over the factory!"

Ogievskij, p. 25.

115

In a factory there lived a lad,
He loved me, a young girl,
To the factory he enticed me,
Gave speeches in secret.
Down the street he walked,
A red flag he carried;
Before I knew this lad,
I had not been in prison.
But as I came to know the lad,
I began to spend time in prison.
Mother began to scold me,

To upbraid me for prison, for hard labor,
Well, mother of mine,
Don't torment me anymore,
I'll tell you a secret—
There is no one dearer to me than him.
A river does not flow to the mountain,
And I will not come back.

Zajcev, p. 138.

116

From the strongholds of Port Arthur,
From the bloody Manchurian fields
A weary crippled soldier
Has returned to his family.
He goes inside, and in the wretched little abode
He recognizes nothing:
Another family has taken shelter there,
Strangers greet him.
And his heart trembles with alarm:
"It's true, I've come back at the wrong time,
Tell me quickly, brothers,
Where is my mother, my family, my little son?"
"Your wife—sit down, rest a bit,
Your wounds must hurt."
"Tell me quickly the whole truth."
"The whole truth? Have courage, soldier!
A crowd of tired workers
Decided to go to the palace
To seek protection, with a petition they went
To the tsar, as to their own father.
Putting on her Sunday clothes,
She also went with the crowd,
And your young wife
Was slashed to death with a saber."
"Where is my mother?"—"To pray at Kazan
Long ago the old lady left here,
Beaten by a Cossack whip,
She barely lived till night."
"And where is my little boy,
My son?"—"Have courage, soldier!
Your son was in Aleksandrovskij Park
And was taken by a bullet from a tree."
"Fate has not taken everything—
There is still my only brother,

A sailor and a handsome lad.
Where is my brother?"—"Have courage, soldier!"
"Can it be true that my brother's no longer alive?"
Perished, perhaps, in the Tsusim Battle?"
"Oh, no, he did not put down his young life
At Tsusim.
He was killed on the Black Sea,
Where their battleship stood,
Because he stood up for truth,
He was killed by his own officer."
Not a word did the soldier mutter,
Only to the sky he raised his eyes—
There was a mighty oath in them
And the threat of future revenge.

Transcribed in 1937. It is a folk rendition of a poem by Ščepkina-Kupernik. The poem was very popular; there are several different transcriptions, done during the Soviet period and earlier (Propp).

II7

On the fourth of the month
The devil brought us
To stop the riot.
Early in the morning they woke us,
Didn't feed us,
Gave us only vodka to drink.
After straightening us up a bit,
They led us to the road
And we set out for Nevskij.
Here in a courtyard they sat us down,
And harshly forbade us
To make a sound.
We didn't feel like an ambush,
Our fellow comrades were annoyed
At such an order.
For a long time, for a little while we sat,
Quiet, not making a sound.
Listen, the detachment says to us:
"Go out to the road
Help the pharoahs [the police],
Klejgel's* has weakened."
In a moment we went out to freedom,
We see—a thousand people.

*Klejgel's—a Petersburg mayor, calling for the dispersal of the demonstration (Tr.).

All the people were making a clamor.
There were free men and soldiers,
Workers and officials—
Everybody was clamoring.
The students began first,
The intelligentsia caught on,
The people began to clamor.
A hammer entered into it;
It flew at an officer,
His blood was spilled.
There was a great commotion,
A fight, a scuffle began,
And we also threw ourselves into it.
We beat the unarmed,
Thrashed and stabbed,
Like on a threshing floor.
Blood flowed in rivers,
Then the tears of many
Poured forth.

Proletarskie poèty, I, pp. 339–340.

118

Brothers, they are driving us far
From our native land—
To the steppes of the Far East,
Yes, oh, will we return from the war?
Is there too little land in Russia
That we have to go to China for it?
If the nobility has taken everything,
Then what do the Japanese have to do with it?
Hunger awaits us, cold awaits us,
Enemy bullets and buckshot.
The hateful command
Has gone mad from too soft a life, and we—
Must answer for their boasting,
Put your heads under the bullets.

Andreev, p. 569. From the archive of the factory Bol'ševik, where this song was spread among the proletariat. It is a soldier song of the Russo-Japanese War (Propp).

119

It is not the grass swaying in the steppes,
It is not the wind rustling in the grove—
A cry brave and powerful is heard,
Ordering us into battle with the foe.

It is not gerfalcons flying down,
Sensing the nearness of corpses—
The working people are taking up arms
To revenge their grandfathers and fathers.

Suffering does not frighten the fighters,
Nor prison, nor the scaffold,
Full of courage, scorn,
Boldly they move forward.

So rise up, powerful force,
Against slavery and chains!
Mete out justice and terrible reprisal:
Tooth for tooth and blood for blood.

Published in *Vperëd* [Forward] 1876, no. 33. It is by an unknown worker and became a popular song. Reprinted in the collection *Revoljucionnaja poèzija* [Revolutionary Poetry] 1954, I, p. 7.

Propp's Sources of Folk Lyrics

Collections of folk lyrics referred to in Propp's text are from the following editions:

Andreev, N. P., ed. *Russkij fol'klor* [Russian Folklore], 2d ed. Moscow-Leningrad, 1938.

Avdeeva, K., *Zapiski i zamečanija o Sibiri. Sočinenie . . . y . . . oj* [Notes and Remarks on Siberia]. Moscow, 1837.

Balakirev, M. *Russkie narodnye pesni* [Russian Folk Songs], *1866, 1900,* ed. E. V. Gippius. Moscow, 1957.

Birjukov, V. P., ed. *Dorevoljucionnyj fol'klor na Urale* [Pre-Revolutionary Folklore in the Urals], I. Sverdlovsk, 1936.

———. *Fol'klor Urala* [Folklore of the Urals], issue I *Istoričeskie predanija, pesni (dooktjabr'skij period)* [Historical Legends, Songs (Pre-October Period)], Čeljabinsk, 1946.

Bogatyrev, ed. *Russkoe narodnoe poètičeskoe tvorčestvo* [Russian Folk Poetry], 2d ed. Moscow, 1956.

Čulkov, M. D., ed. *Sobranie raznyx pesen* [A Collection of Various Songs], St. Petersburg, 1770–1773.

Efimenko, P. S. *Materialy po ètnografii russkogo naselenija Arxangel'skoj gubernii* [Materials on the Ethnography of the Russian Population of the Archangel Province], part 2. *Narodnaja slovesnost'* [Folk Literature]. Moscow, 1878.

Guljaev, ed. *Byliny i pesni Južnoj Sibiri* [Byliny and Songs of Southern Siberia], ed. V. I. Čičerov. Novosibirsk, 1952.

Gurevič, A. V., and L. E. Èliasov, eds. *Staryj fol'klor Pribajkal'ja* [Ancient Folklore of the Pribajkal'], Ulan-udè, 1939.

Gurilev, A., ed. *Izbrannye narodnye russkie pesni* [A Selection of Russian Folk Songs]. Moscow, 1868.

Jakuškin, P. I. *Sočinenija P. I. Jakuškina* [The Works of P. I. Jakuškin]. St. Petersburg, 1884.

Kaševarov, M. S., and K. V. Bogoljubov. *Pesni ural'skogo revoljucionnogo podpol'ja* [Songs of the Ural Revolutionary Underground]. Sverdlovsk, 1935.

Kašin, ed. *Russkie narodnye pesni* [Russian Folk Songs], books 1–3. Moscow, 1833–1834.

Kireevskij, P. V., ed. *Pesni, sobrannye P. V. Kireevskim* [Songs collected by P. V. Kireevskij]. New Series, issue 1. Moscow, 1911; issue 2, pt. 1, Moscow, 1917; part 2, Moscow, 1929.

Leopol'dov, Andrej. *Statističeskoe opisanie Saratovskoj gubernii* [A Statistical Description of the Saratov Province]. St. Petersburg, 1839.

Lopatin, N. M., and N. V. Prokunin. *Sbornik russkix narodnyx liričeskix pesen* [A Collection of Russian Folk Lyrics], pts. 1–2. Moscow, 1889. Republished with introductory article by V. Beljaev. Moscow, 1956.

Ljadov, A., ed. *Sbornik russkix pesen* [A Collection of Russian Songs]. Moscow, 1933.

Maksimov, S. V. *Sibir' i katorga* [Siberia and Penal Servitude], I. St. Petersburg, 1871.

Mordovcev. *Samozvancy i ponizovaja vol'nica* [Pretenders and the Freedman], II. St. Petersburg, 1867.

Mordovceva, A. N., and N. I. Kostomarov, eds. *Russkie narodnye pesni* [Russian folk songs], *Letopisi russkoj literatury i drevnosti, izdavaemye N. Tixonravovyn* [Chronicles of Russian Literature and Antiquity, published by N. Tixonravovyj], IV. Moscow, 1862.

Možarovskij, A. L. *Svjatočnye pesni, igry i gadanija Kazanskoj gubernii* [Wedding Songs, Games, and Fortune Telling in the Kazan Province]. Kazan', 1873.

Nekrasov, I. V. *Pesni russkogo naroda* [Songs of the Russian People]. Moscow, 1902.

Novikova, A. M., ed. *Russkie narodnye pesni* [Russian Folk Songs]. Moscow, 1957.

Ogievskij, M. *Novye èlementy v južno-russkom pesnetvorčestve* [New Elements in South-Russian Songs]. St. Petersburg, 1892.

Pivovarov, A., ed. *Donskie kazač'i pesni* [Don Cossack Songs]. Novočerkassk, 1885.

Pomeranceva, E. V., ed. *Russkoe narodnoe tvorčestvo v Baškirii* [Russian Folklore in Baškir], I. Ufa, 1957.

———. *Pesni i skazki Yaroslavskoj oblasti* [Songs and Fairy Tales of the Yaroslavl' Region], II. Yaroslavl', 1958.

Prač, I., ed. *Sobranie narodnyx russkix pesen* [A Collection of Russian Folk Songs], 1790, ed. V. M. Beljaev. Moscow, 1955.

Proletarskie poèty [Proletarian Poets], Biblioteka poèta, bol'šaja serija, I–III. Leningrad, 1935–1939.

Rimskij-Korsakov, N. A., ed. *Sto russkix narodnyx pesen* [One Hundred Russian Folk Songs]. Moscow-Leningrad, 1951.

Rybinikov, P. N. *Pesni* [Songs], III, ed. A. E. Gruzinskij. 2d ed. Moscow, 1910.

Semevskij, V. *Rabočie na zolotyx promyslax* [Workers in the Gold Mines], I–II. St. Petersburg, 1898.

———. "Iz istorij objazatel'nogo gornogo truda" [From a History of Obligatory Mountain Labor], *Siberskij sbornik* [Siberian Collection] II. Irkutsk, 1897.

Shein, P. V., ed. *Velikorus v svoix pesnjax, obyčajax, verovanijax, skazanijax, legendax, i t.p.* [The Great-Russian in His Songs, Ceremonies, Customs, Beliefs, Tales, Legends, etc.], I, pts. 1–2. St. Petersburg, 1898.

———. "Krepostnoe pravo v narodnoj pesne" [Serfdom in Folk Songs], *Russkaja starina* [Russian Antiquity], nos. 2, 3. (1886).

Šišonko, V., ed. *Otryvki iz narodnogo tvorčestva Permskoj gubernii* [Excerpts from Folkore in the Perm Province]. Perm, 1882.

Sobolevskij, A. I., ed. *Velikorusskie narodnye pesni* [Folk Songs of Great-Russia], I–VII. St. Petersburg, 1895–1902.

Tereščenko, A. V. *Byt russkogo naroda* [The Everyday Life of the Russian People], I–VII. St. Petersburg, 1848.

Tonkov, V. A., ed. *Fol'klor Voronežskoj oblasti* [Folklore of the Voronež Region]. Voronež, 1949.

Varencev, V., ed. *Sbornik pesen Samarskogo kraja* [A Collection of Songs from the Samar Region]. St. Petersburg, 1862.

Vil'boa, ed. *100 russkix pesen* [One hundred Russian Songs]. Moscow, 1894.

Zajcev, I. E. *Narodnoe tvorčestvo Južnogo Urala* [Folklore of the Southern Urals], Issue 1. Čeljabinsk, 1948.

Selected Bibliography

Prepared by June Pachuta and Roberta Reeder

The following bibliography contains the more important collections and studies published in Russia and the West.

I. COLLECTIONS

Balakirev, M., ed. *Russkie narodnye pesni* [Russian Folk Songs], ed. V. Gippius. Moscow, 1957.
Bianchi, Martha. *Russian Lyrics and Cossack Songs Done in English Verse.* New York, 1916.
―――. *Russian Lyrics, Songs of Cossack, Lover, Patriot and Peasant, Done into English Verse.* New York, 1910.
Barsov, E. V. *Pričitanija severnogo kraja* [Laments of the Northern Region]. 3 vols. Moscow, 1872, 1882, 1886.
Bazanov, V. G., and A. P. Razumova. *Russkaja narodno-bytovaja lirika; Pričitanija Severa v zapisjax V. G. Bazanov i A. P. Razumovoj [Russian Lyric Folk Poetry of Everyday Life: Laments of the North, recorded by V. G. Bazanov and A. P. Razumova].* Moscow-Leningrad, 1962.
Čulkov, M. D., ed. *Sobranie raznyx pesen* [A Collection of Various Songs]. St. Petersburg, 1770–1773.
Costello, D. P., and I. P. Foote, eds. *Russian Folk Literature; Skazki, Liricheskie Pesni, Byliny, Istoricheskie Pesni, Dukhovnye Stikhi.* Oxford, 1967.
Kolpakova, N. P., ed. *Lirika russkoj svad'by* [Lyrics of the Russian Wedding]. Leningrad, 1973.
―――. *Russkaja narodnaja bytovaja pesnja* [Russian Folk Songs of Everyday Life]. Moscow-Leningrad, 1962.
Laboulaye, E. *Les Chansons populaires des peuples slaves.* Paris, 1864.
Lopyreva, E. *Liričeskie narodnye pesni* [Lyric Folk Songs]. Leningrad, 1955.
Propp, V. Ja. *Narodnye liričeskie pesni* [Russian Folk Lyrics], 2d ed. Leningrad, 1961.
Pollen, John. *Russian Songs and Lyrics.* London, 1917.
Rimsky-Korsakov, N. A., ed. *Sto russkix narodnyx pesen* [One Hundred Russian Folk Songs]. Moscow-Leningrad, 1951.
Scheftel, George. *Lyrics and Songs from the Russian.* New York, 1925.
Zemcovskij, I. I., ed., *Poèzija krest'janskix prazdnikov* [The Poetry of the Peasant Festivals], 2d ed. Leningrad, 1970.

II. CRITICAL STUDIES

Akimova, T. M. *O poetičeskoj prirode narodnoj liričeskoj pesni* [On the Poetic Nature of the Lyric Folk Song]. Saratov, 1966.
Alekseeva, O. B. "Pesni gornorabočix Urala o pugačëvskom dviženii" [Songs of the Ural Miners on the Pugačëv Rebellion], *Russkij fol'klor* [Russian Folklore], II (Moscow-Leningrad, 1957). Pp. 155–165.
Alexinsky, G. "Slavonic Mythology, *New Larousse Encyclopedia of Mythology.* London, 1968. Pp. 281–299.

184 SELECTED BIBLIOGRAPHY

Anikin, V. P. "Genezis neobrajdovoj liriki" [The Genesis of the Nonritual Lyric], *Russkij fol'klor* [Russian Folklore], XII (Leningrad, 1971): 3–25.
Aristov, N. *Ob istoričeskom značenii russkix razdbojničkix pesen* [On the Historical Significance of the Russian Robber Songs]. Voronež, 1875.
Azadovskij, M. K. *Istorija russkoj fol'kloristiki* [History of Russian Folklore Scholarship], ed. E. V. Pomeranceva. 2 vols. Moscow, 1958–1963.
Bart, H. "Einiges zur Geschichte des russischen Volksleides," *Wissenschaftliche Zeitschrift der Ernst-Moritz-Arndt-Universität Greifswald*, X (1961): 39–43.
Balašov, D. M., and Ju. E. Krasovskaja. *Russkie svadebnye pesni Terskogo berega Belogo morja* [Russian Wedding Songs of the Tersk Shore of the White Sea]. Leningrad, 1969.
Baranov, S. F. *Russkoe narodnoe poètičeskoe tvorčestvo* [Russian Folklore]. Moscow, 1962.
Blum, Jerome. *Lord and Peasant in Russia*. Princeton, 1961.
Bogatyrev, P. G. "O jazyke slavjanskix narodnyx pesen v ego otnošenii k dialektnoj reči" [On the Language of Slavic Folk Songs and its Relation to Dialectal Speech], *Voprosy jazykoznanija*, no. 3 (1962): 75–86.
Brudnyj, V. L. *Obrjady včera i segodnja* [Rituals, Yesterday and Today]. Moscow, 1968.
Chadwick, H. Munro, and N. K. Chadwick. "Russian Oral Literature," *The Growth of Literature*, II. New York, 1936. Pp. 1–296.
Čičerov, V. L. *Russkoe narodnoe tvorčestvo* [Russian Folklore]. Moscow, 1959.
———. *Zimnyj period russkogo zemledel'českogo kalendarija XVI–XIX vekov* [The Winter Period of the Russian Folk Agricultural Calendar from the Sixteenth to Nineteenth Centuries]. Moscow, 1957.
Dobrovolskij, B. M. "Cepnaja strofika russkix narodnyx pesen" [Chain Stanzaic Composition in the Russian Folk Song], *Russkij fol'klor* [Russian Folklore], X (Moscow-Leningrad, 1966): 237–248.
Dunn, Stephen and Ethel. *The Peasants of Central Russia*. New York, 1967.
Eisner, Paul. *Volkslieder der Slawen*. Leipzig, 1926.
Eremina, V. I. "Ob osnovyx ètapax razvitija metafory v narodnoj lirike" [On the Basic Stages of Development of the Metaphor in the Folk Lyric], *Russkaja literature* [Russian Literature], no. 1 (1967): 65–72.
Evgen'eva, A. P. *Očerki po jazyku russkoj ustnoj poèzii* [A Study of the Language of Russian Oral Poetry]. Moscow-Leningrad, 1963.
Hexelschneider, Erhard. "Die russische Volksdichtung in Deutschland bis zur mitte des 19. Jahrhunderts," *Veröffentlichungen des Instituts für Slawistik* XXXIX (1967): 9–29.
Harkins, W. *Bibliography of Slavic Folk Literature*. New York, 1963.
Kozačenko, A. I. "K istorii velikorusskogo svadebnogo obriada" [On the History of Great-Russian Wedding Rites], *Sovetskaja ètnografija* [Soviet Ethnography], no. 1 (Moscow, 1957): 57–71.
Litvin, E. S. "K voprosu o detskom fol'klore" [On the Question of Children's Folklore], *Russkij fol'klor* [Russian Folklore], III (Moscow-Leningrad, 1958): 92–109.
Lineff, Eugenie. *Russian Folk-Songs as Sung by the People and Peasant. Wedding Ceremonies Customary in North and Central Russia*. Chicago, 1893.
Lintur, P. V. "Balladnaja pesnja i obrjadovaja poèzija" [The Ballad and Ritual Poetry], *Russkij fol'klor* [Russian Folklore], X (Moscow-Leningrad, 1966): 228–237.
Longworth, Philip. *The Cossacks*. New York, 1970.
Mahler, Elsa. *Die russischen dörflichen Hochzeitsbräuche*. Berlin, 1960. (Veröf-

fentlichungen der Abteilung für slavische Sprachen und Literaturen des Osteuropa-Instituts [Slavisches Seminar] an der Freien Universität Berlin, XX].

Matossian, Mary. "The Peasant Way of Life," *The Peasant in Nineteenth-Century Russia,* ed. W. S. Vucinich. Stanford, 1968. Pp. 1–41.

Maynard, Sir John. *The Russian Peasant and Other Studies.* New York, 1962.

Melc, M. Ja. *Russkij fol'klor: Bibliografičeskij ukazatel', 1945–1959* [Russian Folklore: Bibliographic Index, 1945–1959]. Leningrad, 1961.

Mirskij, V. V. *Russkaja narodnaja semejnaja pesnja [The Russian Family Folk Song].* Moscow, 1966.

Novikova, A. M. "O strofičeskij kompozicii narodnyx tradicionnyx liričeskix pesen" [On the Stanzaic Composition of Traditional Lyric Folk Songs], *Russkij fol'klor* [Russian Folklore], XII (Leningrad, 1971): 47–55.

Peukert, H. "Zum Bildparallelismus in der russischen Volkslyric," *Studia Slavica Academiae Scientiarum Hungaricae,* XV (1969): 87–102.

Pirkova Jakobson, Svatava. "Slavic Folklore," *Funk and Wagnalls Standard Dictionary of Folklore, Mythology, and Legend,* II. New York, 1950. Pp. 1019–1025.

Poltoratskaja, M. A., ed. *Russkij fol'klor, Xrestomatija, stat'i i kommentarii* [Russian Folklore: Chrestomathy, Articles and Commentaries]. New York, 1964.

Propp, V. Ja. *Russkie agrarnye prazdniki* [Russian Agricultural Festivals]. Leningrad, 1963.

Ralston, W. R. *The Songs of the Russian People.* 1st ed. London, 1872. 2d ed. New York, 1970.

Shein, P. V. *Velikorus v svoix pesnjax, obyčajax, verovanijax, i. t.p.* [The Great-Russian in His Songs, Ceremonies, Customs, Beliefs, Tales, Legends, etc.]. St. Petersburg, 1900–1902.

Šeptaev, L. S. "Pesni razinskogo cikl i pesni o Ermake" [Songs of the Razin Cycle and Songs about Ermak], *Očerki po istorii russkoj literatury* [Essays on the History of Russian Literature]. Leningrad, 1966. Pp. 3–24.

Štokmar, M. P. *Issledovanija v oblasti russkogo narodnog stixosloženija* [Studies on the Versification of Russian Folk Songs]. Moscow, 1952.

Sidel'nikov, V. M. *Poètika russkij narodnoj lirike* [Poetics of the Russian Folk Lyric]. Moscow, 1959.

Sokolov, Y. M. *Russian Folklore,* trans. C. R. Smith. Detroit, 1971.

Sokolova, V. K., "Istoričeskie pesni" [Historical Songs], *Russkoe narodnoe poètičeskoe tvorčestvo* [Russian Folk Poetry], ed. P. T. Bogatyrëv, 2d ed. Moscow, 1956. Pp. 346–407.

Stief, Carl. *Studies in the Russian Historical Song.* Copenhagen, 1953.

Tereščenko, A. V. *Byt russkogo naroda* [Everyday Life of the Russian People]. 7 vols. St. Petersburg, 1898.

The Study of Russian Folklore, ed. Felix Oinas and Stephen Soudakoff. Bloomington, Indiana, 1971.

Tschitscherow, Wladimir. *Russische Volksdichtung,* trans. E. Hexelschneider. Berlin, 1968.

The Village of Viriatino, trans. Sula Benet. New York, 1970.

Tumilevič, T. I. "Donskie predanija o Ermake" [Don Legends about Ermak], *Russkij fol'klor* [Russian Folklore], XIII (Leningrad, 1972): 224–229.

Uxov, P. D. "Postojannye èpitety v bylinax kak sredstvo tipizacii i sozdanija obraza" [The Fixed Epithet in the Byliny as a Means of Typification and the Creation of an Image], *Osnovnye problemy èposa vostočnyx slavjan* [Basic Problems of the Epic of the Eastern Slavs], ed. V. V. Vinogradov. Moscow, 1958. Pp. 158–171.

Vahros, Igor. *Zur Geschichte und Folklore der gross-russischen Sauna* (FFC, 197). Helsinki, 1966.

Zelenin, D. K. *Russische (Ostslavische) Volkskunde.* Berlin, 1927.

Zelnik, Reginald. "The Peasant and the Factory," in *The Peasant in Nineteenth-Century Russia,* ed. W. S. Vucinich. Stanford, 1968. Pp. 158–191.

Index

ROBERTA REEDER, Research Fellow at the Harvard Ukrainian Research Institute, is editor of the *Slavic and East European Newsletter* for the American Folklore Society. She has also been a Research Fellow at the Theater Institute of the Justus Liebig University in Giessen, Germany. She has directed many Slavic festivals and has written and produced performances based on Russian folklore and popular culture.